A QUICK HISTORY OF MATH

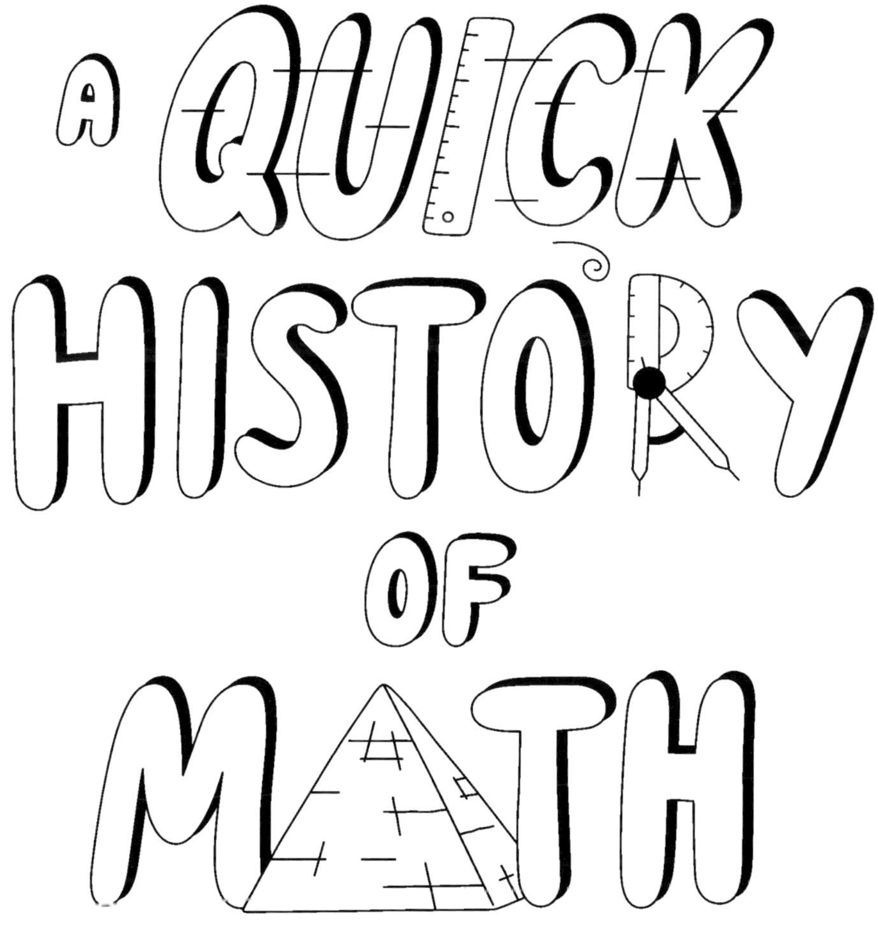

A Quick History of Math

FROM COUNTING CAVEMEN TO COMPUTERS

Clive Gifford and Michael Young

WIDE EYED EDITIONS

CONTENTS

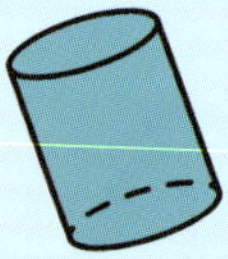

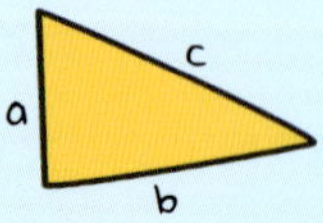

INTRODUCTION

This is a story book about math. In fact, it's the **VERY STORY OF MATH ITSELF.**

You might be thinking—math isn't the sort of thing you find in stories. Math is just numbers, shapes, and really weird equations packed with Xs and Ys. How can you possibly tell a story about that? Surely, math belongs in exercise books, not novels.

WHAT DID YOU LEARN IN MATH CLASS TODAY?

NOT ENOUGH, APPARENTLY. I HAVE TO GO BACK AGAIN TOMORROW!

Well actually, just like the car, chocolate bars, or the light bulb, **MATH IS A HUMAN INVENTION**. OK, some people call it a "discovery" instead, but the point is that the way we use numbers in our everyday lives is shaped by our very human point of view. For example, the fact that our numbers go up in tens is down to most people having ten fingers!

And how we talk about numbers has **CHANGED OVER TIME**. Did you know, for instance, that there was no number zero 1,500 years ago? Or that only 600 years ago in Europe people were still using ROMAN NUMERALS (III, VI, IX) rather than the numbers you know today (3, 6, 9)?

This book takes you on a wild ride through the very human history of math and how it is central to our lives today. You might not realize it, but **YOU RELY ON MATH 24/7**—from divvying up a piping-hot pizza to telling the time to swiping and liking on your smartphone.

So, let's dive in at the start (always a good place to begin any story), with the **LEG BONE** of a baboon...

THE LEBOMBO BONE

Once upon a time, around **43,000** years ago, in a cave in the Lebombo Mountains in Swaziland, southern Africa, a prehistoric human needed to count something (or keep count of something).

So, they cut **29** notches in a **BABOON'S LEG BONE**.

This object was rediscovered in the 1970s and is now the oldest surviving mathematical object in the world. Experts believe it is the first known way of recording numbers and is called a **TALLY STICK**.

A prehistoric person would cut a notch in the **BONE** using a sharpened stone for every one of an item they wanted to count.

So how did those experts in the 1970s know it was a **TALLY STICK?**

Well, because tally sticks continued to be used in the same way throughout history. Archaeologists have discovered **HUNDREDS** of more recent tally sticks from the Middle East, Australasia, and Africa. Some were carved deer antlers or wolf **BONES**, others were small tree branches. One of the most notable was the 20–22,000-year-old Ishango bone. It, too, was a baboon's leg bone carved with notches.

Animals were probably pretty unhappy about the invention of the tally stick.

Keeping a tally using sticks or other memory aids continued for thousands of years, even though people didn't have actual numbers (like 1, 7, and 88) to count with.

KEEPING TRACK

No numbers? No bother. **TALLY STICKS** meant that a person could just glance and match the number of notches to the number of the thing they counted, such as fish caught, or how many family members they had... well, most of the time.

Tally sticks, *er*, stuck around for ages. In **Medieval Europe**, they were used instead of money for debts and taxes. The stick was notched, then **SP LIT** lengthways in two, so both parties had a record of the amount owed.

In fact, the British government only stopped using split tally sticks in 1826. When they burnt their vast tally stick collection eight years later, it didn't end well...

...the fire burned down the Houses of Parliament!

Tally sticks weren't the only things people used. Some used piles of **STONES, SEA SHELLS**, or even leaves to keep count. The latter option probably wasn't the wisest...

Ancient Incas used strands of alpaca or llama wool with knots in different positions and colors to show amounts.

These were called **QUIPUS** or **TALKING KNOTS**.

For counting small quantities, of course, there was another option—not knots or notches.

CAN YOU PUT YOUR FINGER ON IT?

FINGERS AND TOES

Early peoples often counted using what was close to **HAND**. And let's face it, nothing is closer to hand than, er, your hands.

Okay, your nose is closer to your eyes, but there's only one of it, so it won't get you very far in the old counting game. By the way, if you can count two noses, you're either cross-eyed or need a visit to the doctors, pronto.

Where were we? Ah, yes. If they weren't using tally sticks, shells, or knotted ropes, prehistoric peoples were using their **FINGERS** (and toes) to count with. (And by the way, the word for finger, **"DIGIT,"** is also the word used to describe a single whole number, such as the 8 in 182 or the 7 in 3,674.)

Most people have a full quota of four fingers and thumb on each hand... so it's no surprise that counting in fives or tens became popular.

How to count to 12 with your fingers

Tens are still popular, and form our **DECIMAL** number system of ones, tens, hundreds, and thousands.

Some peoples used their hands in different ways. In parts of prehistoric Asia, people counted in twelves.

They used their thumb to point to one of the three parts of their four fingers.

However, larger amounts and **serious** math demand more than just fingers and toes to work with.

So, around **10,000** years ago, when some people stopped hunting, gathering, and wandering around, the need for numbers **GREW**—along with the crops that they began to farm.

HOME NUMBER

Peoples in Mesopotamia (present-day Iraq) were among the first to settle down, call one place home, and farm to survive. Suddenly, there was **MUCH, MUCH MORE** that needed counting—from days left in the growing season to herd numbers and the amount of crops grown.

The first number systems began with one (a sensible choice) and then repeated it to make other numbers. **BIG** bundles of ones could get unwieldy, so new symbols were invented to stand for **LARGER** numbers.

More than **5,000** years ago, the Sumerians and, a little later, the **BABYLONIANS** (both from Mesopotamia) started writing things down. They used a reed pressed into soft clay to make wedge-shaped imprints. The clay was then baked in the sun to make rock-hard tablets.

The **BABYLONIANS** used a vertical wedge symbol for the number one and a horizontal wedge for ten.

Collections of these wedges were used to write numbers down, for example:
VVVV = 4, <VV = 12 and, **<<<VVV = 33.**

All the way up to 60, which was written in the same way as the symbol for 1, but one place value over...

BABYLONIAN NUMBERS

1	11	21	31	41	51
2	12	22	32	42	52
3	13	23	33	43	53
4	14	24	34	44	54
5	15	25	35	45	55
6	16	26	36	46	56
7	17	27	37	47	57
8	18	28	38	48	58
9	19	29	39	49	59
10	20	30	40	50	60

BABYLONIAN BASES

The Babylonians counted in **SIXTIES**, but their numbers knew their place and each place had a different value.

CONFUSED? I don't blame you!

I was baffled until I thought about our own number system, which is called **BASE 10** and also uses **PLACE VALUES**.

BASE 10 has ten different digits (0 to 9). When you want to go large—bigger than 9—you add an extra column or place. Voilà! You can now count from 10 up to 99... and adding a further place lets you get from 100 to 999. Simple.

In base 10, each new place is worth **10 TIMES** more than the previous one.

For example, 66 is written with a 6 in the ones column, and a 6 in the tens column.

The Babylonians' **BASE 60** worked in the same way, only their digits went from 1 to 59 before they added a new place. Each new place was worth 60 times more. So, where we deal with ones, tens, and hundreds, the Babylonians worked with ones, 60s, and 3,600s.

Place values are great at allowing **BIG** amounts to be written with small numbers. For example, 3 3 3 in base 60 equals 10,983.

3,600s	60s	1s
3	3	3

The Babylonians didn't have zero so they often left a space, otherwise 3,000 and 3 would appear the same.

Base 60 might sound a bit **BONKERS,** but it's still with us today. You use it whenever you tell the time (60 seconds to a minute, 3,600 seconds to an hour). Most civilizations that came after the Babylonians, though, counted in tens—including the EPIC EGYPTIANS.

COUNT LIKE AN EGYPTIAN

While the Babylonians played with tricky sixties, a few hundred miles to the west, pyramid-packed, temple-tastic ANCIENT EGYPT was a math mecca.

The Egyptians made many math breakthroughs... when they weren't busy building, farming, keeping baboons as pets, or pulling brains out through nostrils to help turn dead bodies into mummies!

Numbers and words were written using a picture-based language of symbols called **HIEROGLYPHS**. Each symbol was chiseled in stone or inked on papyrus (beaten n' dried Nile river reeds) by people called scribes. These brainiacs needed great memories with over **700 DIFFERENT SYMBOLS** to learn. Most ordinary ancient Egyptians couldn't read or write.

ANCIENT EGYPTIAN numbers were basic base 10, but they had no special symbols for 2, 3, 4, 5, 6, 7, 8, or 9. And no zero, in fact. The answer to 3 x 2 would be shown as six vertical strokes, each representing 1.

6 = ||||||

But their hieroglyphs got more interesting as the numbers **GREW** and **GREW**...

10 was shown as a heel bone

100 was a coil of rope

1,000 a lotus plant.

10,000 was drawn as a finger

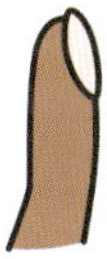

100,000 was a tadpole or frog

With no place values, numbers could get very **L O N G**, very quickly. As an Egyptian scribe, you would **NOT** want to be writing 999,999...

HUH, THANKS A MILLION!

ANCIENT EGYPT was a **BIG**, rich kingdom. And huge armies, crops, taxes, and wages sometimes required **BIG** numbers. In the land of the pharaohs, writing 999,999 needed nine of each of the six hieroglyph symbols, making a number 54 hieroglyphs long. Sheesh.

The ancient Egyptians produced the first known symbol for a million. In comparison, the biggest number the ancient Greeks (who followed the Egyptians) had was a **"MYRIAD,"** which equaled 10,000. puny!

The hieroglyph for one million depicted one of Egypt's most ancient gods, **HEH** or **HUH**.

UH?

No, **HUH**—
the god of long life.
He was shown with
his arms stretched out.

While we're looking at terrific hieroglyphics, did you know the Egyptians used a pair of legs for plus and minus signs? If the legs were walking in the direction that the number was written, they were a plus. If they were walking away from the number, they were a minus.

Interestingly, the Egyptians also had a symbol for **INFINITY**, although we doubt they used it in their math. The shen ring was a circle that depicted eternity (forever).

The hieroglyph for the shen ring is a tied loop of rope

FRACTIOUS ABOUT FRACTIONS

Managing a big kingdom meant not only needing **BIG** numbers, but also more ways to divide them up. Fractions were a **BIG DEAL** in ancient Egypt—one of the first places to use them.

Most of what we know about math in ancient Egypt comes from just two fragile pieces of PAPYRUS. One, the 3,600-year-old Rhind Papyrus, is packed full of math problems and $\frac{81}{87}$ ths of them are about fractions.

Fractions make it easier to **DIVIDE UP** things such as bread for workers, land for farmers, or treasures for the pharaoh's favorites. We write them like this:

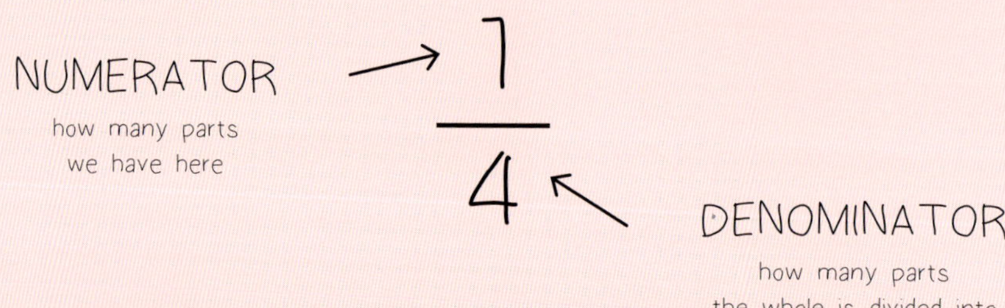

So far, so good, but the awesome ancient Egyptians did make life hard for themselves in $\frac{4}{2}$ (that's two) ways.

Firstly, they only used unit fractions where the **NUMERATOR** (the top number) is always a one. So, you'd never see seven-ninths near the Nile.

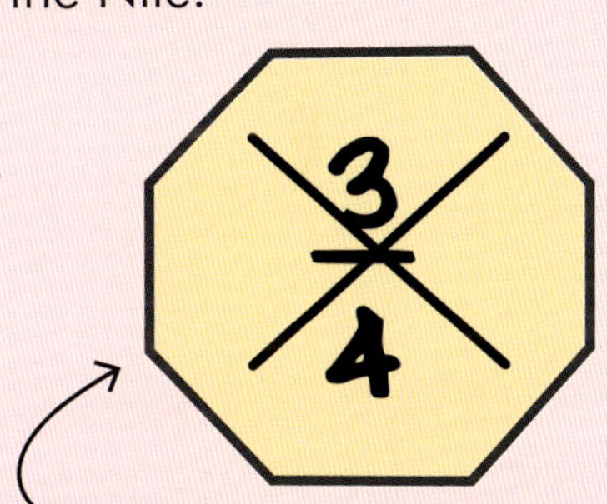

Not allowed in ancient Egypt

Secondly, fractions used together had to be different. You couldn't get to $\frac{3}{4}$ by putting $\frac{1}{4}+\frac{1}{4}+\frac{1}{4}$.

OH DEARY ME, NO.

It had to be $\frac{1}{2}+\frac{1}{4}$, which is pretty straightforward, but other fractions got messy quickly.

For example, $\frac{6}{7}$ would be $\frac{1}{2}+\frac{1}{3}+\frac{1}{42}$ while $\frac{2}{29}$ would equal: $\frac{1}{24}+\frac{1}{58}+\frac{1}{174}+\frac{1}{232}$

TRICKY!

But not as tricky as trying to build a pyramid... that called for some **MONUMENTAL** math.

MONUMENTAL MATH

Evidence of the ancient Egyptians' mathematical prowess can still be seen today. After all, you don't build **PERFECT PYRAMIDS**, one of which was the world's tallest structure for 3,500 years, without knowing a fair bit about math. Fortunately, for the ancient Egyptians, they did!

They were able to find the area of triangles and squares and knew how to calculate a pyramid's volume. They also used **GEOMETRY** to measure the gradient (steepness) of a slope—crucial in lining up the faces of a pyramid.

They also needed to multiply large numbers, but the way they did it was pretty **FUNKY**.

They used something called **SUCCESSIVE DOUBLING**. Are you ready?

A scribe would write out a table with powers of two (1, 2, 4, 8, 16, and so on) in the first column. In the second column, they'd double one of the numbers to be multiplied again... and again... and again.

So, for 21 x 16, you'd get:

After a short nap (probably), the scribe would pick numbers in the first column that added up to 21, then trace across and add the second column numbers together to get the answer.

You're probably pleased that you don't have to learn to do multiplication in this way at school—it's a bit **COMPLICATED**. But it goes to show that, like with counting and number systems, people did math very differently in other times and places.

THOSE GEOMETRIC GREEKS

Almost 3,000 years ago, ANCIENT GREECE emerged as the brightest civilization around the Mediterranean. Its many small city-states like Sparta and Athens often bickered and battled, but in between got some serious math done.

The GREEKS borrowed and built on the mathematics of societies that came before them, such as the Egyptians.

But compared to the practical Egyptians, the Greeks *loved* knowledge for its own sake. They were the first to seek out and test **UNIVERSAL RULES** about the math behind shapes, lines, areas, and distances.

This geeky Greek way of coming up with ideas about how they thought math worked and then finding a way to **PROVE** it was very important and influential—we still do math in this way today.

When a universal mathematical rule has been proven to always work, it's called a **THEOREM**. Some of the Greeks' earliest theorems were about shapes, in the area of math known as **GEOMETRY**, from the Greek words for "Earth" and "measuring."

Geometry comes in two branches: **PLANE** and **SOLID**.

If you're feeling flat, **PLANE GEOMETRY** is for you—it's all about lines and two-dimensional (2D) objects such as circles, squares, triangles, and trapeziums.

For solid 3D action, you'll need **SOLID GEOMETRY**—it's the math of three-dimensional objects, including cubes, cylinders, and spheres.

THROWING SHAPES

The cube was one of **FIVE SPECIAL SOLIDS** identified by ancient Greek geometry geeks. Each was made up of flat surfaces or faces all of the same size. The same number of faces met at each vertex (what solids have instead of corners).

THE FAB FIVE ARE:

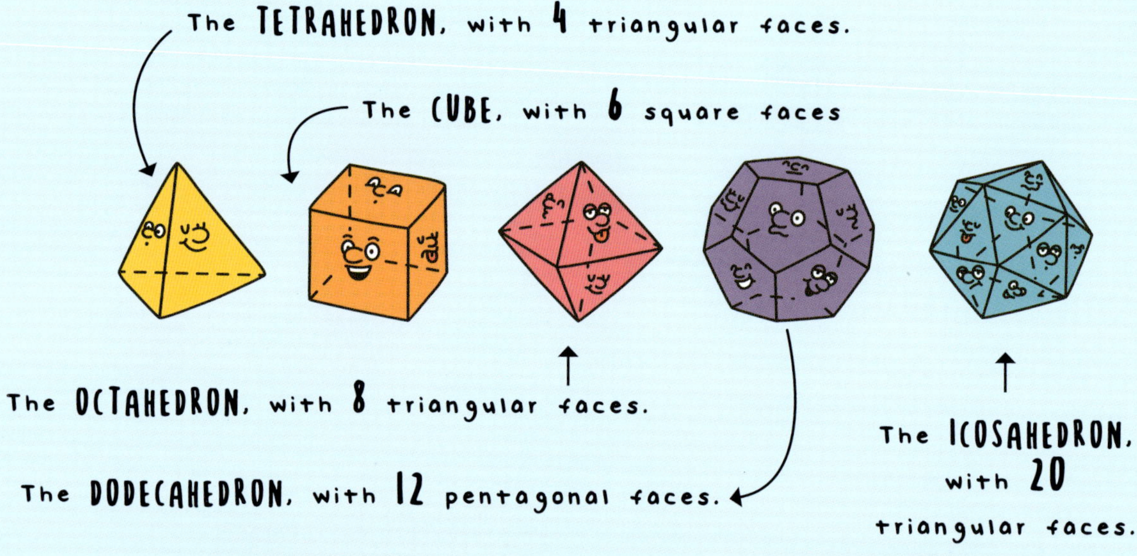

They were known as the **PLATONIC SOLIDS** after top philosopher, Plato. His school, The Academy, only let students in if they were marvelous at the math of shapes.

Ancient Greeks also studied solids with different-sized flat faces such as **CUBOIDS** and **PRISMS**. That's not all. Solids with curved faces such as **CONES, SPHERES,** and **CYLINDERS**, also grabbed their attention. The earliest known female mathematician, Hypatia, who was born around 350 CE, wrote about the mathematics of cones, as well as being a famous teacher of philosophy.

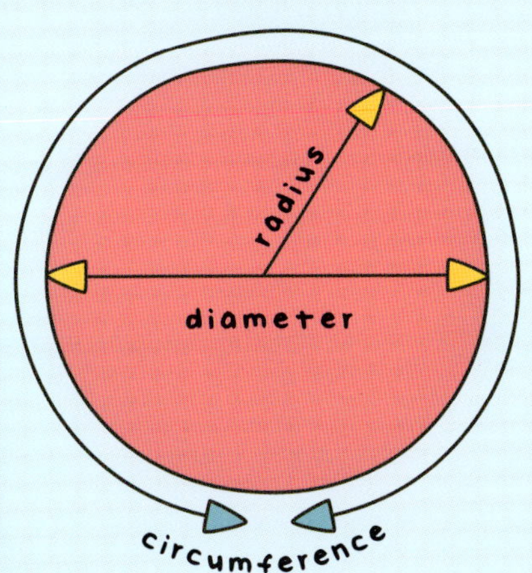

CONES and **CYLINDERS** in a roundabout way bring us back to **CIRCLES**, one of the shapes that most fascinated the geometric Greeks. They noted how every part of a circle's **CIRCUMFERENCE** (its outer edge) was the same distance away from the center. This distance is known as the **RADIUS** and when it's used to help find a circle's area, we're talking Pi time!

EASY AS PI

The GREEKS (and others before them) discovered a handy **RATIO** (more about these on page 40) between the circumference and the diameter of a circle. This ratio is a **CONSTANT**—it never varies no matter the circle's size.

It's named after the Greek letter, **PI** or **π**, and is about **3.14**. A circle's circumference is **about** 3.14 times bigger than its diameter.

Now, "about" doesn't sound very mathematical and precise, but Pi is what's called an **IRRATIONAL NUMBER**—a number with no end.

The ancient EGYPTIANS had a crack at working out Pi and got to just over 3.16. Not bad, but ancient GREEKS like Archimedes got closer. Math men and women since have gone π-crazy, using supercomputers to calculate it to a number 20,000 million digits long. I know, I know. You'd think they'd have something better to do.

WHAT IS PI USEFUL FOR? Well, you can use it to find the area of a circle by squaring the circle's radius (multiplying it by itself) then multiplying that figure by Pi. The formula for this is written $A = \pi r^2$

So, let's say the radius of a circle is 3 inches. Like this circle, right here.

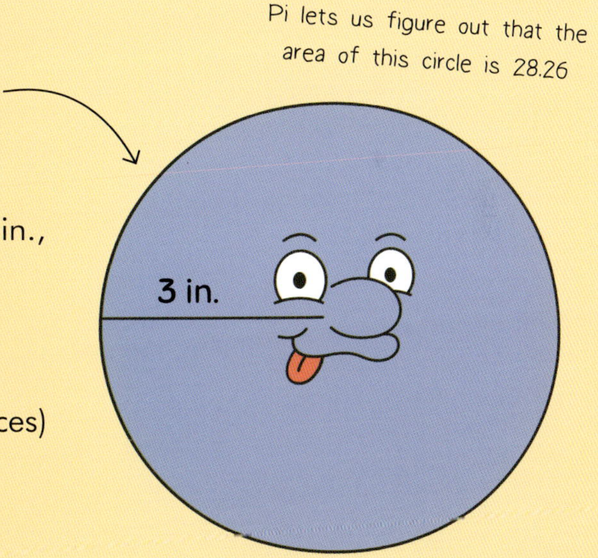

Pi lets us figure out that the area of this circle is 28.26

3 in.

We know the formula is: Area $= \pi r^2$
In our example here, the radius is 3 in., so we write:

Area $= \pi \times 3^2$.
We know that Pi (to two decimal places) is 3.14, so that means the

Area $= 3.14 \times (3 \times 3)$.
That gives us the answer. The area of our circle $= 28.26$ in.^{2} (to two decimal places).

EASY AS... PI! Want more π ? How about Pi-thagoras—sorry, Pythagoras: the first really great Greek geometer.

LIVING BY NUMBERS

When it comes to superstar Greek mathematicians, **PYTHAGORAS** is definitely A-list. You've probably heard of the **THEOREM** that carries his name, even if you aren't totally sure what it is (more on that in a minute). Pythagoras opened a school in Croton, a Greek colony of Italy, around 530BCE. His many students and followers, the Pythagoreans, were an odd bunch. They had the motto, "**ALL IS NUMBER.**"

The Pythagoreans really lived by numbers and believed they explained the world. They considered the **NUMBER TEN** so perfect that they never gathered in groups larger than that.

They also thought of odd numbers as male and even numbers as female. For the Pythagoreans, numbers had symbolic meanings, so 5 (3 + 2) was the symbol of marriage—we're talking **serious** math nerds here.

They had some ***strange***, non-number, beliefs as well, including never eating beans or peeing while facing the Sun!

The Pythagoreans discovered that the three internal angles of a triangle always added up to 180°. They also learned how to find the length of the longest side (called the **"HYPOTENUSE"**) of a right-angled triangle—using math's first fantastically famous theorem—**PYTHAGORAS' THEOREM**, of course.

To use this theorem, you measure the length of the triangle's two shorter sides and square them. When added together, they equal the longest side squared. It's written as:

$$a^2 + b^2 = c^2$$

a^2, b^2 ↑ two shorter sides; c^2 ↑ longest side (the hypotenuse)

But hold on a minute. What is all this square number business, anyway?

IT'S HIP TO BE SQUARE

A **SQUARE NUMBER** is the answer when a number is multiplied by itself, such as 3 x 3 = 9 or 10 x 10 = 100.

So, in these examples, **9** and **100** are square numbers.

Another way of saying the same thing is that it is the first number "to the **POWER OF 2**." This means the same thing—a number multiplied by itself. But it is written as the number with a small 2 above it, such as 3^2 (meaning three "to the power of two," which is 9) or 10^2 (meaning ten "to the power of two," which is 100).

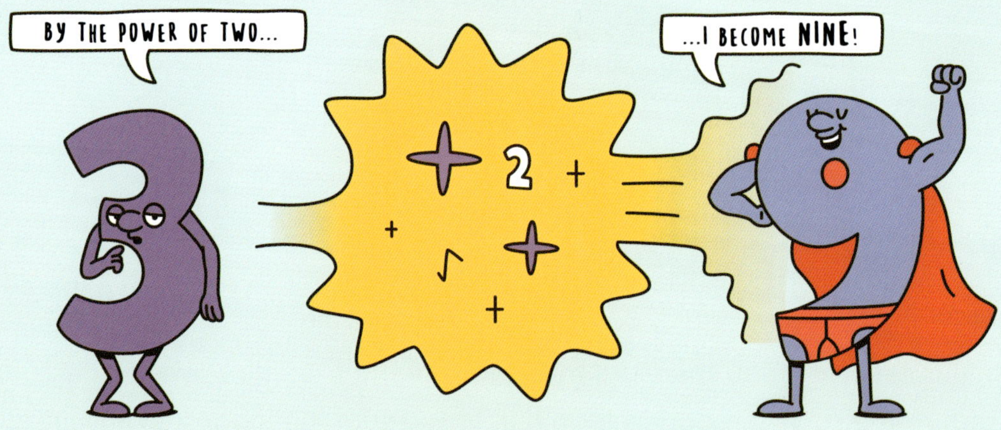

It was those way-back Babylonians who were the first to produce tables of **SQUARE NUMBERS**. These instantly give you the area of a square—handy for both building and dividing up areas of farmland.

Now, **SQUARE ROOTS** are kind of the opposite to square numbers. They're the number that is multiplied by itself to make a square. So, remember our examples 9 and 100 above? If 9 is the square number, then 3 is the square root. If 100 is the square number, 10 is the square root.

Figuring out the square root of 9 or 100 is not too hard, but most square roots are tricky, and are not **WHOLE NUMBERS**. So these days, most mathematicians reach for the "square root (√)" button on their calculator.

By the way, did you know there's an unofficial holiday called **SQUARE ROOT DAY**? It's whenever the day and month are the square root of the last two digits of the year. The next one's on 5/5/2025.

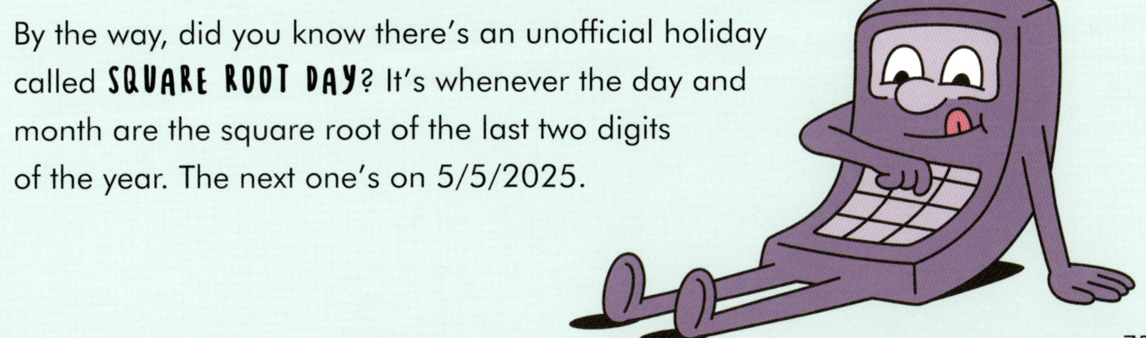

PROVE IT!

Remember we talked about universal rules and theorems back on pages 26–27? The ancient Greeks were the first people to really separate out **MATH** from **MAGIC, RELIGION,** or just one person's point of view.

The Greeks tested their math out scientifically, checking that their theorems worked in all cases. **"PROOFS"** are what we call the explanations of why a math theorem or idea is true. They are often built from **"AXIOMS"**—starting facts known to be correct.

The **FIRST KNOWN PROOF** was by a Greek mathematician called THALES OF MILETUS around 2,600 years ago. He proved that a diameter line always divides a circle into two equal parts.

Some things are easier to prove than others. Pythagoras' theorem, for instance, can be proven just by reaching for a ruler.

1. Draw a right-angled triangle like the one below.

2. Check what Pythagoras' theorem would give you for the hypotenuse, remember $a^2 + b^2 = c^2$

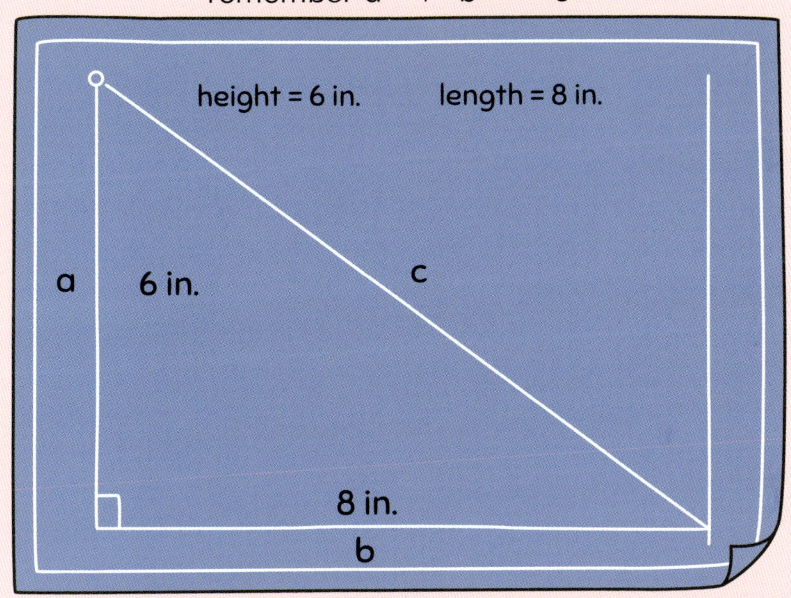

$6x6 + 8x8 = 100 \rightarrow \sqrt{100} = 10.$

3. Measure the hypotenuse (long diagonal side) with a ruler. It should equal 10 in., proving the theorem.

Other proofs, of course, took a lot more work. Some even run to thousands of pages.

One great Greek gathered up a collection of axioms and proofs to publish the first **MEGA MATH BOOK** around 300 BCE. That math man was Euclid.

WHO ARE EU... CLID?

You'd think the author of the world's most influential nonfiction book would be a dead-famous mega-celeb... but you'd be wrong.

Little is known about **EUCLID**, other than he lived in Alexandria and published the book, *Elements*, around 300 BCE. This monster volume was packed with 465 different theorems and proofs.

It started with some axioms and points that Euclid thought were true, such as "**PARALLEL LINES WILL NEVER MEET.**" and "**A STRAIGHT LINE CAN BE DRAWN JOINING ANY TWO POINTS.**" These were used as building blocks for other math in the book.

Elements was widely read and is still used by top math bods 2,000 years later. It's believed to be the second most reprinted book of all time, only behind the Bible!

His incredible impact on the subject led to Euclid having the nickname **"FATHER OF GEOMETRY,"** because his work was essential to the discoveries of other famous mathematicians such as Johannes Kepler and Isaac Newton (read more about him on page 88), thousands of years after Euclid's death.

Over $\frac{1}{2}$ the book was packed with geometry. It included how to calculate the **VOLUMES** of various solids. Euclid showed how a cone has a third of the volume of a cylinder of the same size. The volume of a cylinder and a cone can be compared using **RATIOS**—one of the many subjects in Euclid's book.

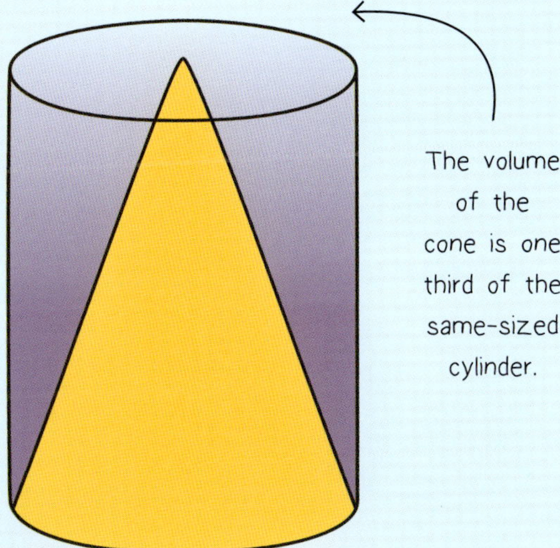

IN A RELATIONSHIP

A **RATIO** shows the relationship between two (or more) numbers, such as the **LENGTH** to the **WIDTH** of a shape, or the amounts of items in a mixture. Ratios are written with a colon (:) between the values, like this **A:B**.

Ratios can be multiplied by a number to scale their amounts up or down while keeping their **PROPORTIONS** the same—handy in recipes, maps, and engineering.

In fact, if you ever want to bake a delicious cake without referring to a recipe, you just need to remember this very simple ratio, **1:1:1:1**. These refer to the amounts of **SELF-RAISING FLOUR**, **SUGAR**, **BUTTER**, and **EGGS**. Just weigh your eggs first, then add the same weight of each of the other three ingredients. Mix the batter together, and bake in a medium oven until risen and golden. Voilà!

One other ratio, **1:1.618*** proved particularly pleasing to Euclid and the Greeks, not because it is a cake recipe, but because throughout history people have admired its proportions.

The Greeks named this ratio **PHI** or **φ** after Phidas, the sculptor who helped design the beautiful Parthenon temple in Athens. We call **PHI** the **GOLDEN** or **DIVINE RATIO** and it's been used in many famous buildings and paintings. Today's credit cards are **"GOLDEN RECTANGLES"** with two sides 1.618 times longer than the others.

Credit cards use the golden ratio

Euclid noted a fun feature of golden rectangles. When you cut a square off one end of a golden rectangle, the bit left behind makes another golden rectangle. This process can be repeated again and again!

Start with a golden rectangle...

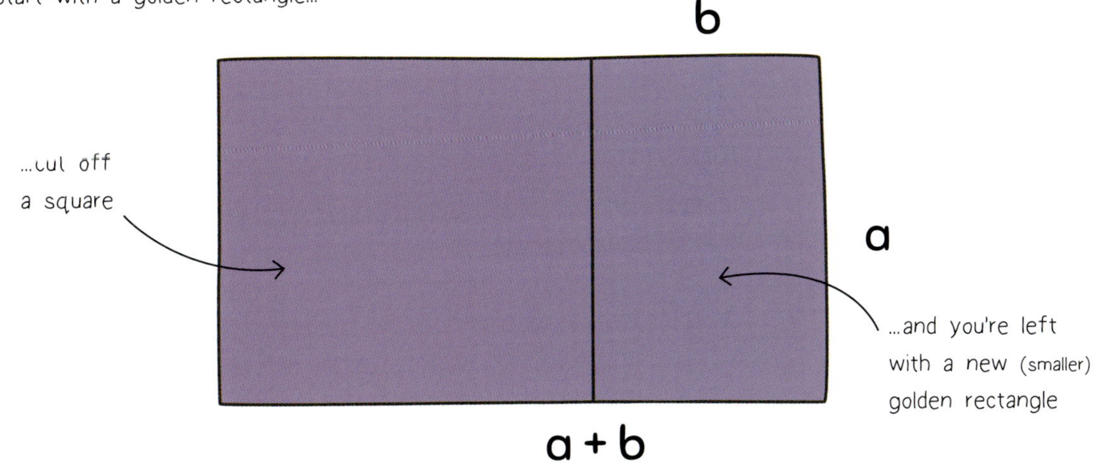

*This is shortened. Like Pi, the golden ratio goes on and on forever.

PARADOXES

Let's just step backward in time again for a moment, before Euclid, before the weirdo Pythagoreans, and before Plato, to meet another GREEK dude called **ZENO**. He was a philosopher born around 495 BCE, and one of the things that really got him excited was **PARADOXES**. What's a **PARADOX**? It's something that contradicts itself or makes no logical sense. Here's one:

THE SECOND SENTENCE IS FALSE. THE FIRST SENTENCE IS TRUE.

Which is correct? You cannot tell. One statement contradicts the other.

ZENO thought up a bunch of mathematical paradoxes, and they will really fry your brain. Several of them helped explore the idea of unlimited amounts in mathematics—what we now call **INFINITY**.

Imagine that you want to walk from your **HOUSE** (point A) to the **STORE** (point B). Well, first you have to get **HALFWAY** to the store, right? You can't get all the way to the store without first getting halfway to the store. So far, so good.

But then, you still have to get half of the remaining way, before you'll reach the store. Continuing like this, there will always be some small distance left between you and the store, and you'll **NEVER** actually get there.

You can write this down as a number series, like this:

$$\frac{1}{2} + \frac{1}{4} + \frac{1}{8} + \frac{1}{16} + \ldots \text{ etc.}$$

When you think about it like this, getting from a point A (your house) to point B (the store) is **IMPOSSIBLE**! The math seems to make sense... but our experience tells us that it is definitely possible to walk to the store (and even arrive, buy some candy, and walk back). It's a **PARADOX**!

PRIME TIME

Whizzing forward in time again to around 236 BCE and we meet yet another Greek brainiac, **ERATOSTHENES**. He was made the librarian of the famous Library of Alexandria, which attempted to house every text ever written at the time. One of Eratosthenes' mathematical inventions was a way to find **PRIME NUMBERS**.

Prime numbers are whole numbers that can only be divided by themselves or the number one. For example, 17 cannot be divided by anything except 1 and 17. An example that is **NOT** a prime number is 9, because it can be divided by 1, 9, and 3. The lowest prime (and the only even prime number) is 2.

As for the highest... well, the sky's the limit. In 2018, a mathematician figured out a prime number which ran to 24,862,048 digits. If each digit was written out 14mm wide, the whole prime number would stretch from **LONDON** to **PARIS**.

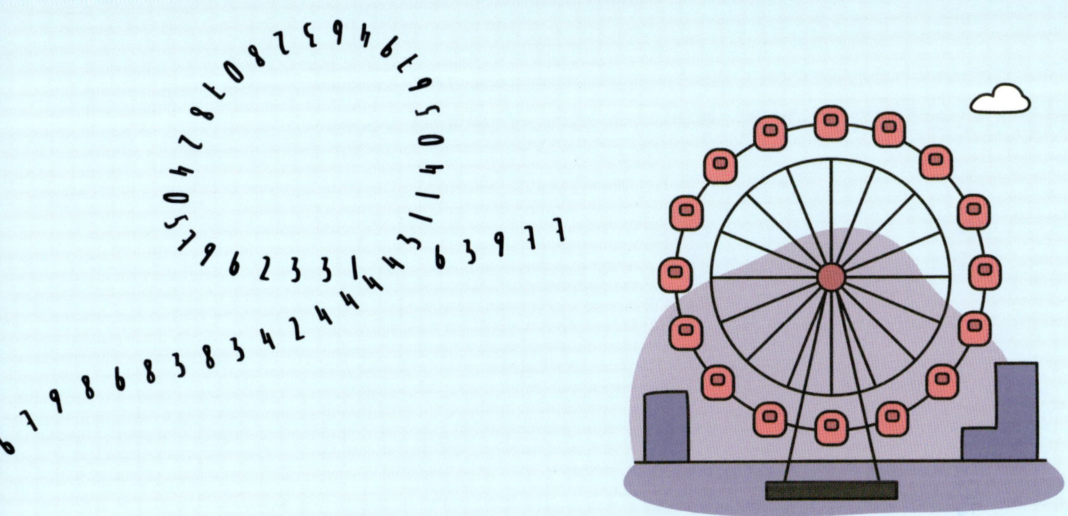

Eratosthenes didn't quite get that far, but his invention, called **"THE SIEVE OF ERATOSTHENES"** is a handy way to find all the prime numbers between 1 and 100.

- First, write a grid from 2 to 100.
- Remove all numbers you can divide by 2 (except 2 itself), then 3, then 5, and finally, 7.
- The numbers left behind, all 25 of them, are primes.

NIFTY, eh? But you should see what Eratosthenes did next. In 240BCE, he took on the world...

ERATOSTHENES VS. THE EARTH

ERATOSTHENES was well-traveled for his time. Born in Libya, he'd studied in GREECE and worked in EGYPT. This was only a tiny fraction of the planet, yet without trekking around it or flying high above it, our plucky librarian measured the entire Earth and got it 99% right.

Eratosthenes knew about Syene, far south of Alexandria. There, once a year, (midday on midsummer's day, seeing as you asked), the Sun was directly overhead and its rays headed straight down a well without casting a **SHADOW**.

Eratosthenes measured the shadow cast by a tall tower where he lived in Alexandria on midsummer's day. Using **GEOMETRY**, he calculated the angle of the Sun's rays to be 7.2°.

With 360° in a circle, 7.2° is $\frac{1}{50}$ th of its circumference. By multiplying by 50 the distance between Syene and Alexandria (which he gauged as about 500 miles) Eratosthenes calculated the Earth's circumference as 24,850 miles. **GENIUS!**

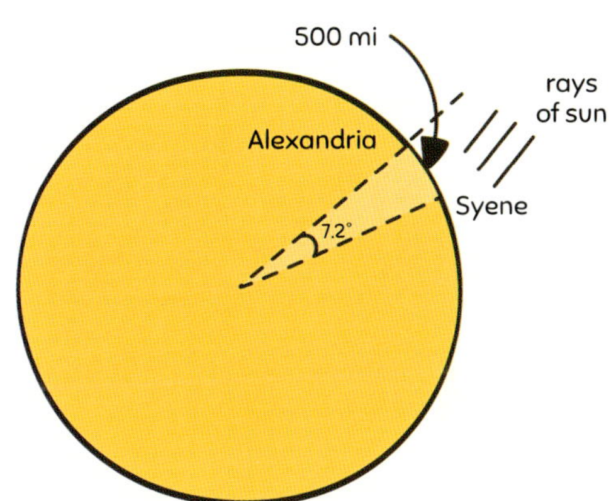

Using his mathematical insights into the size and shape of the Earth, **ERATOSTHENES** also pretty much invented geography! He was the first person to actually use the term "geography," (meaning "writing about the Earth" in Greek), and he pioneered other concepts, such as describing the Earth in terms of climate zones: **FREEZING ZONES** around the poles, temperate zones below, and a hot zone around the equator.

Eratosthenes was good pals with other key thinkers of the era, too. One of his pen pals, Archimedes, was also a math maestro, but known best for a bath he took...

THE NAKED TRUTH

"EUREKA!" cried the streaker as he ran through his home city of Syracuse overjoyed at figuring out how to measure an odd-shaped object's volume. This great GREEK thinker had leapt from his bath after noting how the amount of water pushed away by an object placed in water (his body) equaled the object's volume.

When he wasn't streaking, Archimedes was an inventor and an A* mathematician.

He used the power of levers and pulleys to build large cranes and war machines to defend his city. He invented the **"ARCHIMEDES SCREW,"** a device for moving water or grain from a low point to a high point.

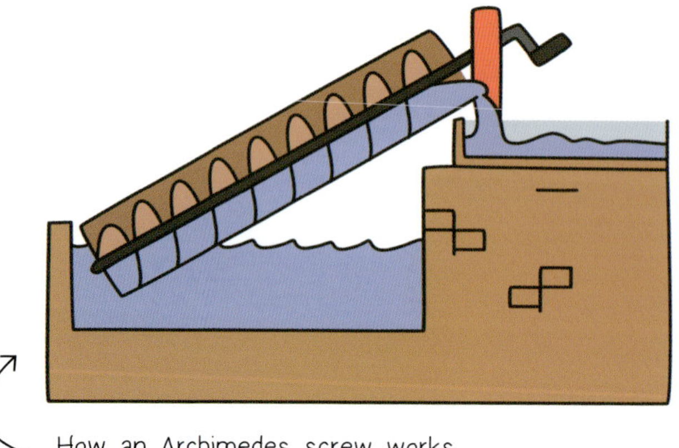

How an Archimedes screw works

A sphere the same size as a cylinder has two-thirds the cylinder's volume

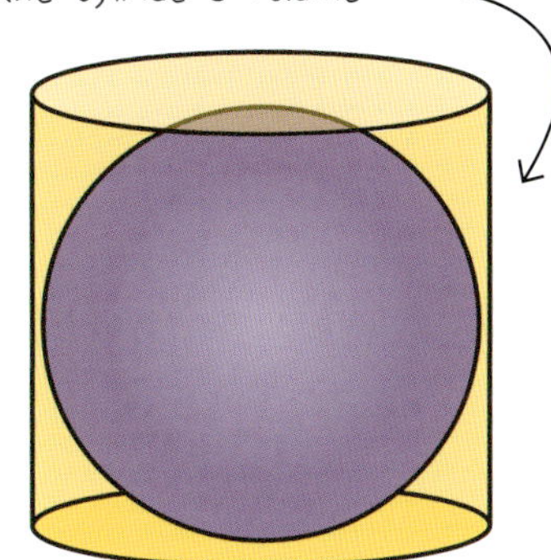

He measured **PI** more accurately than anyone before and learned how to calculate the surface areas of many solids. He found that a sphere the same size as a cylinder had two-thirds the cylinder's volume.

He also developed some big, **BIG** numbers in order to try to count the grains of sand in the universe. What? You heard me! He got up to 10 to the power of 63 (10^{63})—that's a 10 followed by 63 zeros.

10,000,000,000,000,000,000,000,000,000,000,000,000,000,000,000,000,000,000,000,000,000,000

Archimedes remained math-mad to the very end, which came in 212 BCE...
...when the ROMANS invaded Syracuse.

Soldiers were given instructions to **"SPARE THE MATHEMATICIAN,"** such was his fame, but unfortunately one Roman didn't get the memo.

ROAMING WITH THE ROMANS

Syracuse wasn't the only place the ancient ROMANS invaded. The ROMANS built the **BIGGEST** empire the world had ever seen, but they didn't conquer math, particularly.

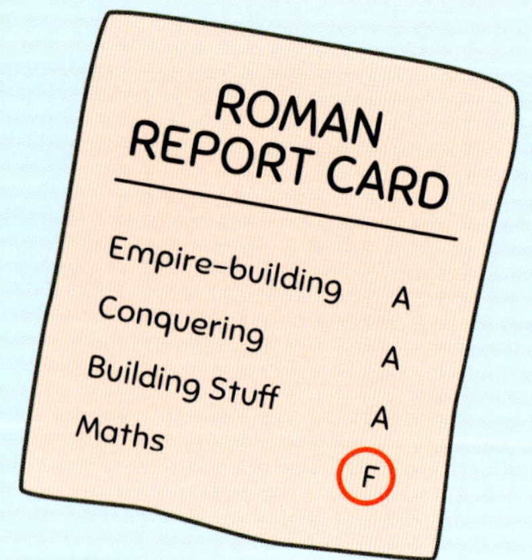

ROMAN REPORT CARD

Empire-building	A
Conquering	A
Building Stuff	A
Maths	F

Why? It's a bit of a head-scratcher to be honest... but here are three possible reasons...

1) We know the ROMANS took a lot of good stuff from the ancient GREEKS, including a lot of their **GEOMETRY,** which helped them plan epic buildings, roads, and structures.

II) The ROMAN number system wasn't very helpful. For a start, there was **NO ZERO** or **PLACE SYSTEM** and they used letters for numbers, like this...

I=1 V=5 X=10 L=50 C=100 D=500 M=1,000

As a result, numbers grew very large. You needed 8 Roman numerals just to write 88 (LXXXVIII) and 14 to write 2,888 (MMDCCCLXXXVIII). Sheesh!

Also, when a letter is placed before another that has a higher value, the smaller figure is taken away. So, IX = 9 (10 – 1) and XL = 40 (50 – 10). **CONFUSING.**

III) Perhaps the ROMANS were just too busy doing stuff and killing people to do much thinking, unlike the philosophical GREEKS. The ROMAN EMPIRE expanded very quickly, requiring an awful lot of fighting and new road building, so maybe they just had less spare time for sitting around pondering new math theorems.

At any rate, while the ROMANS were battling everyone they came across and looning around with letters for numbers, the clever Chinese were doing some seriously impressive math of their own.

THE ART OF MATHEMATICS

When they weren't inventing paper, fireworks, umbrellas, wheelbarrows, and many other useful things, the ancient **Chinese** were very busy mastering math.

The **Chinese** worked with negative numbers in trade and business, long before mathematicians in the West believed that **NEGATIVE NUMBERS** could exist. They color-coded negative numbers black and positive numbers red. If after buying, selling, trading, and doing all your sums, you were left with red numbers, you were in the money. **YAY!**

Interestingly, in today's business world, the color coding's the other way round. Companies strive to be **"IN THE BLACK"** meaning they have more money than debts.

Where was I? Ah, yes. China needed people to run its large empire, so officials had to learn lots of real-world math.

Famous ancient textbooks such as *The Nine Chapters on the Mathematical Art* were packed with practical math, such as how to use ratios to collect taxes for the emperor and how volumes could measure the size of a crop harvest or how much space a grain store contained.

One of the very first Chinese math books, 2,200 years ago, was written on 200 strips of bamboo. Called Suàn shù shū, meaning *The Writings on Reckonings*, it showed how to take fractions away from each other and showed remainders in division as fractions. For example, dividing 16 goats among 3 farmers gave each farmer 5 goats with the remainder, 1, split into three $\frac{1}{3}$ portions.

MAGIC SQUARES

As well as working on very serious and useful math, the Chinese conjured up a fun mathematical invention, the magic square. These are puzzle grids, and the simplest contain nine numbers in a 3 x 3 grid. Each row, column, and diagonal in the square all add up to the same sum—this is known as the **MAGIC CONSTANT**.

The ancient Chinese loved a good legend and pinned the discovery of magic squares on the mythical Emperor Yu. Over 4,000 years ago, Emperor Yu is said to have been walking along the banks of the Luo River. Suddenly, a **MAGICAL TURTLE** emerged from the water, with strange markings on the nine panels of its shell.

The emperor realized that the markings formed the numbers of a **MAGIC SQUARE**, and declared that the pattern had magical importance, symbolizing the harmony of the universe.

Can you create a new **MAGIC SQUARE**? Have a go at drawing a 3x3 grid and filling it out so every row, column and diagonal add up to the same sum. It's not easy!

In time, magic squares spread from China, to India, and beyond. Mathematicians tested their mathematical mettle and constructed 4x4, 5x5, or even larger squares. In 1514, the German artist Albrecht Dürer included an extra-special 4x4 square in one of his engravings. As well as the rows, columns, and diagonals adding up to a **MAGIC CONSTANT** of 34, the four outer corners, the four numbers in each quarter, and the four central numbers do too. Wow!

While people in China and India puzzled over magic squares, the **MIGHTY MAYA** on the other side of the planet were doing math with dots n' dashes.

MAYA MATH

The Maya bossed **CENTRAL AMERICA**, peaking 250–900 CE, when they created towering temples, sprawling cities, stunning art, and advances in astronomy and math.

The Maya used all their fingers and toes (providing they hadn't been chopped off as a punishment) to count in **BASE 20**. (Remember, we count in base 10, so we only have the different digits 1 to 9, and to count higher we have to add another place value.)

The Maya had 19 different digits, each made up of **DASHES** and **DOTS**. These probably stemmed from sticks and stones used earlier.

The dots in their digits were worth one, and the dashes were worth five. The smaller bits were written above the larger, so was 6 (a dot meaning 1 sitting on top of a dash meaning 5) and equalled 13 (2 dashes of 5 + 3 dots of 1).

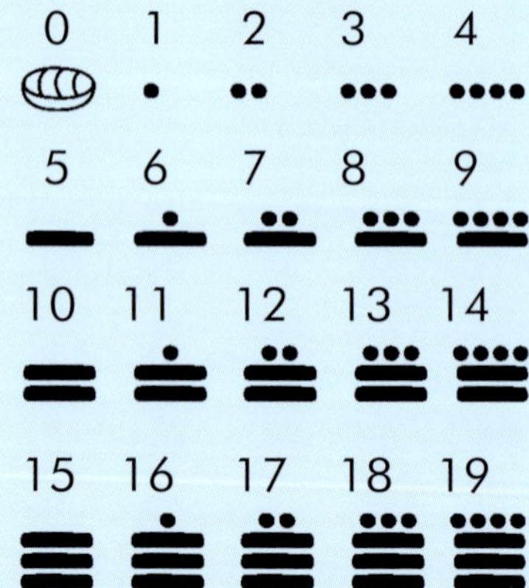

The Maya also had bigger numbers covered. When they reached 20, they added a new place value, just like we do. However, they wrote their numbers from top to bottom rather than from left to right. For example, 2,139 would

read 2

1

3

9 in the Maya system... ...like this.

So, the higher the place, the **LARGER** the number.

In **BASE 20**, these are the place values:

160,000
8,000
400
20
1

To write 200,000, all the Maya needed was a single **DOT** and one **DASH**. The dot went in the 160,000s and the dash in the 8,000s (i.e. 1 x 160,000) + (5 x 8,000) = 200,000. Genius.

160,000	
8,000	
400	
20	
1	

But what did the Maya use these **BIG** numbers for?

OH, MAYA DAYS

Set on your 7-days-a-week, 52-weeks-a-year routine? Better take a deep breath… It's about to get madly Maya around here.

The Maya used **ASTRONOMY** to build complex **CALENDARS** and plotted Earth's year as lasting 365.242 days—pretty much spot on and all without telescopes.

Not content with one **CALENDAR**, often carved on giant stone discs, the Maya used three, plus other cycles of days and even a calendar for the planet Venus. That's just plain greedy, isn't it?

The shortest, **TZOLK'IN**, lasted 260 days, while **HAAB** contained 18 months, each 20 days long. Five extra **UAYEB** days were added and also thought of as unlucky—best stay in and wash your hair.

Tzolk'in and Haab reached the same point once every 18,980 days (52 years). Whoopee! But it wasn't the Maya's longest period.

The Maya's Grand Cycle lasted 9,360,000 days and some doom mongers feared the *End Of The World* in December 2012 when the cycle was thought to finish. Some people believed that Nibiru, a planet allegedly discovered by the Sumerians, was going to hit the Earth and cause the *apocalypse*. Obviously that didn't happen.

The Maya kept track of their calendars using **DOTS**, **DASHES**, and one extra symbol—a **SNAIL SHELL**, which recorded empty places in a number. So, 2012 would be written:

▬ = 2000 (5 x 400)

(shell) = nothing

(dots and dashes) = 12

The Maya didn't think of their shell as an actual number like zero became, but hey, that proved not to be the end of the world...

BIG FAT ZERO

It's astonishing to think that the Maya, the ancient GREEKS, and some other great civilizations made **GIANT** strides in math yet never came up with the number **ZERO**!

It took brainy Indian scholars to turn nothing into something. One of them, Brahmagupta, defined zero as the result of taking away a number from itself around 628 CE.

He was the first to devise rules for treating zero as a number in its own right. These included:

- When zero is added or taken away, the number stays as it is.
- Any number multiplied by zero becomes zero.

It wasn't just a coincidence that an Indian developed the idea of **ZERO** as a number in its own right. In the West, after the advent of Christianity, religious leaders believed that **GOD** is in everything that exists, and so anything that represents nothing is the *devil's work*. This put the kibosh on any work on the idea of zero for a long time in Western mathematics.

In Buddhist philosophy, on the other hand, the idea of **"NOTHINGNESS,"** and emptying the mind, is key to achieving **NIRVANA** (a kind of heavenly state of existence), so Indian mathematicians were already inclined to think a lot about nothing.

ZERO is not a positive number (and it's not a negative number, either) but it sure had a positive impact on math. It worked brilliantly with long numbers needing place holders, and is a crucial part of **CALCULUS** (see pages 88–89) and binary numbers (see pages 98–99), which have underpinned modern engineering and technology. The philosophical concept of zero is ultimately what has given us **COMPUTERS**, the **INTERNET**, and **SMARTPHONES**!

The concept of "nothing" is essential to both Buddhist philosophy and modern technology.

NUMBERING UP

Zero is not the only number that began life in **INDIA**. In fact, all the numbers you use began life in India and developed from Brahmi numerals first written down more than 2,000 years ago. These morphed into the **HINDU-ARABIC** number systems, with its separate symbols for the numbers, 1 to 9, with zero joining the party a little later.

Brahmi ↓		𑁧	𑁨	𑁩	𑁪	𑁫	𑁬	𑁭	𑁮	𑁯
Hindu ↓	०	१	२	३	४	५	६	७	८	९

This number system helped India become a center of math excellence during 400–1,000 CE and one of its brightest stars was **ARYABHATA**, born in 476 CE. Speaking of stars, this Hindu numbers merchant was obsessed with **SPACE** and used all sorts of math to investigate the night sky and Earth.

He used geometry to get Earth's circumference right to within 0.2%. **BIG TICK.** ✓

He also measured Earth's day accurately to within 0.09 seconds. **EVEN BIGGER TICK.** ✓

ARYABHATA showed how to solve equations with more than one unknown number and used a method involving dividing numbers by smaller and smaller amounts. It was called kuttaka—meaning "the pulverizer," and broke up difficult equations into tiny bits. **SMASHING**!

A century or two later, the works of Aryabhata, Brahmagupta, and other Indian math geniuses had spread into the **ARABIC** world, along with the numbers they used. At that time, an Islamic empire stretched from the edge of India, across the Middle East, into Africa and Europe.

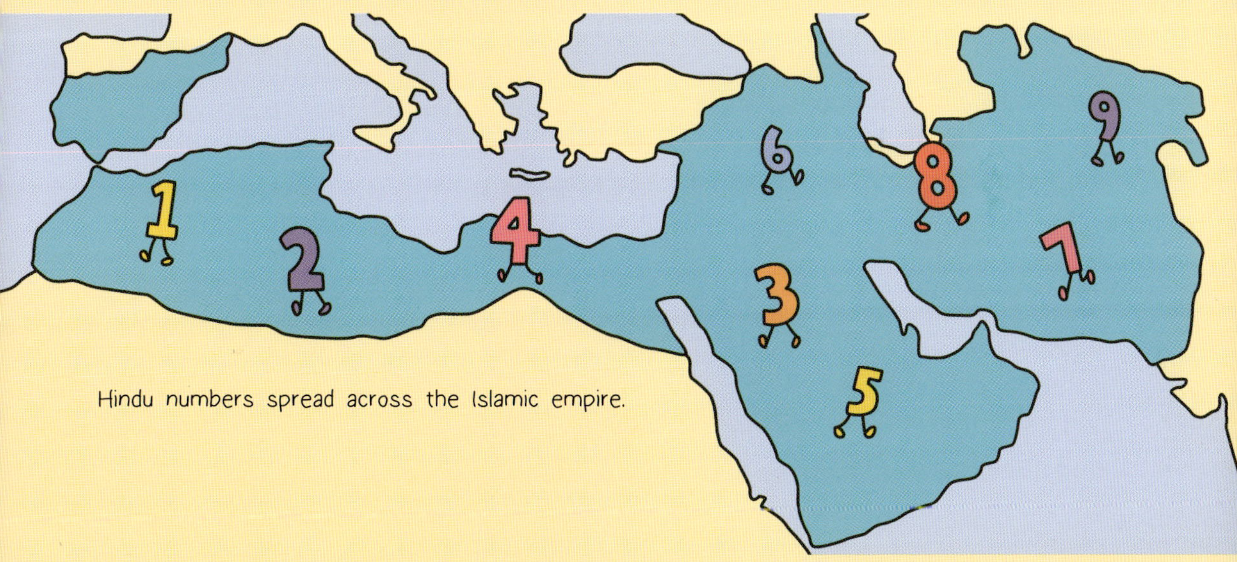

Hindu numbers spread across the Islamic empire.

This helped kick off a golden age of **PHILOSOPHY**, **ART**, and **SCIENCE**, including some momentous Muslim math breakthroughs. But just before we get into those, let's take a look at one further, Indian-inspired innovation that's frankly **IRRATIONAL**...

THINKING IRRATIONALLY

Around 500 CE, Aryabhata also came up with a really accurate figure for Pi, but didn't jump for joy as he also realized he would never get Pi perfectly right. The reason? Because Pi goes on forever. It was one of the first times in history where a mathematician 'fessed up to there being "**IRRATIONAL NUMBERS**."

What on earth is an irrational number? Well, **RATIONAL** numbers are numbers that can be shown as **FRACTIONS**. So 9, for example, can be expressed (as math people say) as the fraction $\frac{18}{2}$.

It's not only **WHOLE** numbers that can be rational. **NON-WHOLE** numbers can be rational as well, as long as they can be expressed (there's that word again) as a fraction. For example, 2.25 forms the fraction $\frac{9}{4}$.

IRRATIONAL NUMBERS, on the other hand, cannot be expressed as fractions. Instead, they form a stream of decimal places with no repeating pattern that stretches on **FOREVER**.

The square root of 3 (√3) is an irrational number, and so is the golden ratio.

Ancient Greeks simply refused to believe that irrational numbers existed. One member of Pythagoras' school, Hippasus, stumbled across irrational numbers when trying to find the **SQUARE ROOT OF 2**. Not that it did him any good. Some say that he drowned at sea. Was he pushed? We don't know.

But we do know that math took great leaps at another school, this time in **BAGHDAD**, further to the East.

THE HOUSE OF WISDOM

Baghdad (in modern-day Iraq) was a gleaming new city in the 8th Century, when a great library and school known as **Dār al-Ḥikma**, meaning the "**House of Wisdom**," was established. It contained lots of rare books and scrolls and attracted the brightest minds around.

Among the scholars at the **House of Wisdom** were the **Banū Mūsā** brothers, Ahmed, Hassan, and Muhammad. They wrote important books on **GEOMETRY**, surveyed land and canals, and designed over 100 outrageous **MACHINES**, which they wrote about in a book called *The Book of Ingenious Devices*. Their inventions included a conical valve (the kind that we have in our taps today) and a robot-like mechanical flute player powered by steam—one of the first ever programmable machines.

Another super-important figure at the **House of Wisdom** was the astronomer and mathematician **Muḥammad ibn Mūsā al-Khwārizmī**. We believe that he became the director of the House of Wisdom around 820 BCE and had a **BIG** impact.

Firstly, he urged the Muslim world to adopt the **0–9** number system from India (which became known as **HINDU-ARABIC** as a result).

Secondly, he created a series of steps and instructions to solve problems such as multiplying and dividing large numbers really quickly. These were named "**ALGORITHMS**" in his honor and are created by coders when making computer programs today.

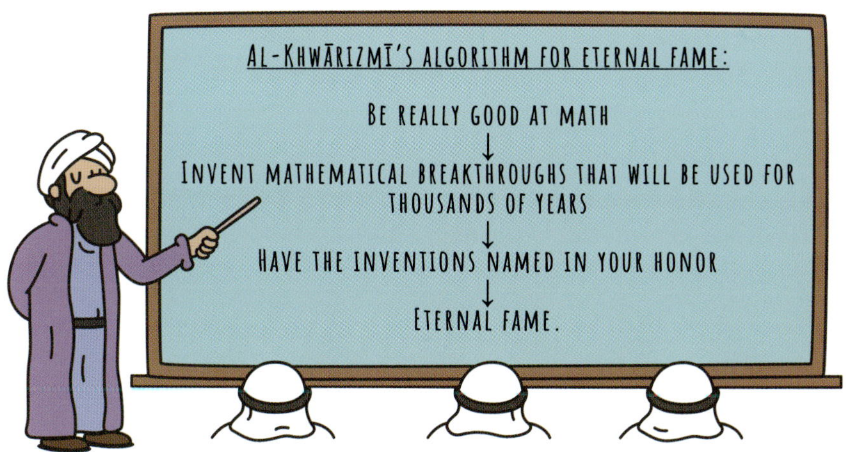

Thirdly (boy, was he busy), he produced amazing work on equations and **ALGEBRA** (more on that in a mo), so important that the very word "**ALGEBRA**" comes from part of his book's title in Arabic, al-jabr.*

*The book on algebra was called (deep breath), *The Compendious Book on Calculation by Completion and Balancing*. Phew!

ALGEBRAAAARGH!

OK, algebra is known to make some people quiver and go "**AAARGH!**" But it's simply a set of rules and methods in math used to discover unknown values. Our Arabic algebra pal, **al-Khwārizmī** called an unknown value **SHAY**, meaning "*the thing*." Centuries later, letters like x and y were used instead.

You can show a simple, spooky sum of three witches and four zombies as 3 + 4 = 7. But if you don't know a value in the equation (such as the number of witches), algebra helps you work it out...

x + 4 = 7

By the way, al-Khwārizmī didn't actually use the equal sign as it wasn't invented for another 700 years, by Welshman Robert Recorde in 1557.

But ignoring the zombies and witches for a moment, what's an **EQUATION**? A simple way to understand it is like a set of old-fashioned balancing scales. The **EQUAL SIGN** in the equation is the middle point of the scale.

In order for an equation to be correct, both sides must be in **BALANCE**, and equal the same amount. Algebra helps you work out unknown values by keeping the scales (your equation) balanced.

Even though in our *Halloweeny* example we don't know how many witches there are, we can work it out as long as we treat both sides of the equation the same. To find x, we start by magicking away the +4 (the zombies) on the left-hand side.

We don't know how many witches there are, so first we zzzzap the zombies away...

But to keep the scale **BALANCED**, we have to do the same on the right-hand side. Taking away 4 on the right-hand side leaves us with 3. Therefore, we know that $\mathbf{x = 3}$.

...then we zzzap the same number of vampires, and that tells us the remaining number on each side is 3!

So algebra will tell you the number of witches, but not what their names are. You'll have to figure out for yourself which witch is which!

SPIES AND SYMMETRY

It wasn't all algebra among Arab mathematicians. Around 850 CE, one scholar at the **House of Wisdom**, called Al-Kindi, developed a math technique to crack **SECRET CODES** used by spies.

Called **FREQUENCY ANALYSIS**, it measured how often different letters in a language typically appear. In English, for example, the letter "e" appears 12.7% of the time while "z" is a rarity, only turning up with a frequency of 0.07%.

By analyzing **CODED MESSAGES** where letters have been swapped, Al-Kindi's work allowed spies and spymasters to crack the code, put the correct letters in their place, and read **SECRET MESSAGES** quickly.

Other Muslim mathematicians were fascinated not by spying but by **SYMMETRY**. This part of geometry is about one shape becoming exactly like another when it is moved in some way. A **TWO-DIMENSIONAL** (2D) shape is **SYMMETRICAL** if a line (the line of symmetry) can be drawn through it so that both parts of the shape on either side of the line look exactly the same.

Different shapes may have one or more lines of symmetry—or none. In the case of circles, the number is **INFINITE**!

Muslim artists followed the rules of symmetry when decorating walls and floors of palaces and temples with tiles that didn't overlap or leave gaps. These are called **TESSELLATIONS** and form repeating patterns.

Although there appear to be **MILLIONS** of different designs, Muslim mathematicians and artists found that there are only 17 different basic patterns that are **SYMMETRICAL**. All 17 were used to decorate the **ALHAMBRA**, a spectacular 14th Century palace in Spain, just one example of magnificent Muslim math that reached Europe.

MATH HEADS WEST

While Indian, Chinese, and Arabic mathematicians were busy calculating and innovating, in the 700–1,100s, much of **EUROPE** was making do with old thinking and **ROMAN NUMERALS**... in between bashing itself senseless in battles.

Gradually, the good work of Eastern math maestros headed West to **EUROPE**, often carried by sailors and traders, or translated by Islamic scribes, particularly those in Toledo in **SPAIN**. The scribes would often work in pairs, one reading and translating the Arabic math out loud and the other writing it down.

The works translated included the Arabic numerals for **0–9**, some of which began taking on the shapes we're familiar with today.

In some parts of Europe, though, the new numbers and math did **NOT** go down well...

The Italian city of Florence, for instance, **BANNED ZERO** and other Arabic numbers in 1299. Other places feared algebra and thought of zero as *black magic*.

Ordinary people, few of whom could read or write, struggled with change and the idea of **ZERO** and **PLACE VALUES**. Two centuries later, many Europeans were still using Roman numerals, and it was only the arrival of the **PRINTING PRESS** that made the new numerals popular throughout the continent.

Some math-mad Europeans saw the value in Arabic numbers straight away and how they allowed **FASTER CALCULATIONS**. And one of their biggest champions was a young mathematician, Leonardo of Pisa, also known as **FIBONACCI**.

FAB FIBONACCI

As a young man, Fibonacci traveled with his dad to the Middle East where he was amazed at how **FAST** Arabic number-crunchers performed math using **ALGEBRA** and **0–9** numbers. He returned home excited to tell the rest of Europe.

In 1202, he wrote a book, *Liber Abaci*, all about algebra and the Hindu-Arabic number system. The book was widely copied and inspired many to move away from Roman numerals, especially merchants and traders who saw **QUICKER MATH** as **QUICKER CASH**!

The book also introduced a never-ending sequence of numbers (the **FIBONACCI SEQUENCE**) that has fascinated people ever since.

Each number in the sequence is created by adding up the two previous numbers.

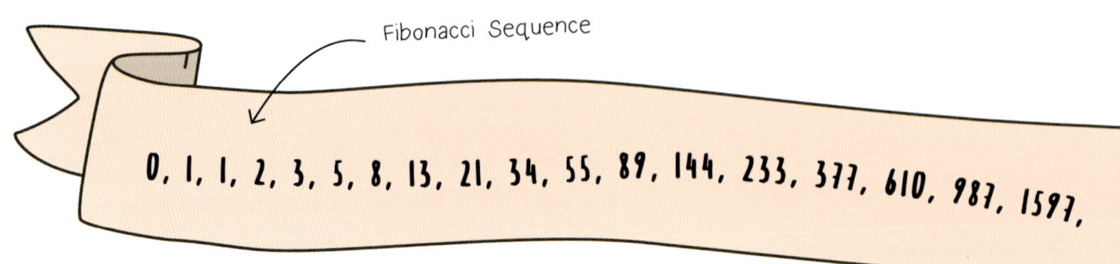

The **FIBONACCI SEQUENCE** is found throughout nature in the design of spirals found in some seed cones, shells, and flower buds. Fibonacci numbers also feature in the numbers of daisy petals, but to demonstrate his number sequence, Fibonacci just rabbited on...

He used a four-part riddle about **FAST-BREEDING BUNNIES**:

1. You start with a pair of baby bunnies at the start of January.
2. Each pair take a month to grow into adults.
3. Each pair of adults produce a pair of baby bunnies every month.
4. How many pairs of rabbits by the end of December?

With **12 MONTHS** in a year, all you have to do is head to the 12th number in the sequence after zero to find the answer, which is **144 PAIRS**. If you'd started with 8 pairs, count 12 places from 8 in the sequence and you'd end up with 3,194 rabbits (1,597 pairs)—a real **BUNNY BONANZA**. Think of all the lettuce they'd get through.

2584, 4181, 6765, 10946, 17711, 28657, 46368, 75025, 121393, 196418, 317811...

EXPONENTIAL POTENTIAL

The thing about Fibonacci's sequence is the numbers get really **BIG**, really ***quickly***. Number sequences like that can be tricky to get your head around. For example, if I were to ask you whether you'd rather have **ONE MILLION DOLLARS**, or the sum of a penny doubled every day for a month, what would you go for?

MOST people choose the **MILLION BUCKS**, it seems like a safe bet. But you might be surprised to learn that if you opted for the penny, you'd be **$5,368,709.12** richer at the end of 30 days!

That's because our **LUCKY PENNY** is growing exponentially. An **EXPONENT** is just a quick way of saying you want to multiply a number by itself a particular number of times. We've actually already met an exponent in this book, but it had a special name. Remember **SQUARE NUMBERS** from page 34? We know that 4^2 means 4 x 4. It's four "to the power of two," or two fours multiplied together. Another word for that little ^{2} is the "exponent."

If you wanted to, you could write four to the power of five, or 4 x 4 x 4 x 4 x 4 as 4^5.

Here, 5 is the exponent. Can you figure out how much 4^5 is?*

ARCHIMEDES dabbled in exponents. So did **al-Khwārizmī**, who used the term **KAHB** for numbers to the power of 3 (such as 10^3). Kahb is where we get the term "**CUBED**" from. Exponents started being used more and more in the 16th Century.

*The answer is 1,024.

JOLLY LOGARITHMS

Europe in the 1400s and 1500s underwent a **BOOM** in new ideas and sciences. Astronomy, navigation by ships, trade, and many sciences all required math—lots of it—but they didn't have calculators. People were crying out for ways to ***speed up*** their calculations.

Luckily, Scottish mathematician **John Napier** had a solution. He was an odd guy, with goth-black clothing, a **PET ROOSTER**, and a **BLACK SPIDER** that he kept with him at all times in a small box (as you do).

Napier invented **LOGARITHMS**, which are really another way of thinking about **EXPONENTS**. We know that ^{5} is the exponent when we write $4^5 = 1{,}024$.

A **LOGARITHM** contains the same information, but organized in a different way. To write it as a logarithm, we'd write:

$\log_4(1{,}024) = 5$

Err, you might be thinking: **SO WHAT**? What does that have to do with calculations for astronomy and navigation and whatnot?

The other thing **John Napier** did, along with his pal Henry Briggs, was make huuuuge tables of logarithms. In order to do the kind of **MASSIVE MULTIPLICATIONS** needed in these new sciences, it was much easier to look up logarithms in Napier's tables and add them together. In this way, tough x and ÷ tasks were turned into far quicker and easier + and - sums.

Then, in 1617, Napier produced a series of rods covered in numbers (gothically nicknamed "**Napier's Bones**"). People could line these up to multiply numbers, a little like a calculator built by another math genius over in France.

PASCAL'S PATTERNS

Born in France in 1623, **BLAISE PASCAL** was one of those annoyingly smart child geniuses you sometimes hear about—you know, the type that gives regular kids a bad name.

While he was a teenager, he built one of the world's **FIRST MECHANICAL CALCULATORS** (the Pascaline), read (and understood!) all of Euclid's *Elements*, and had a geometry theorem named after him. Good for him.

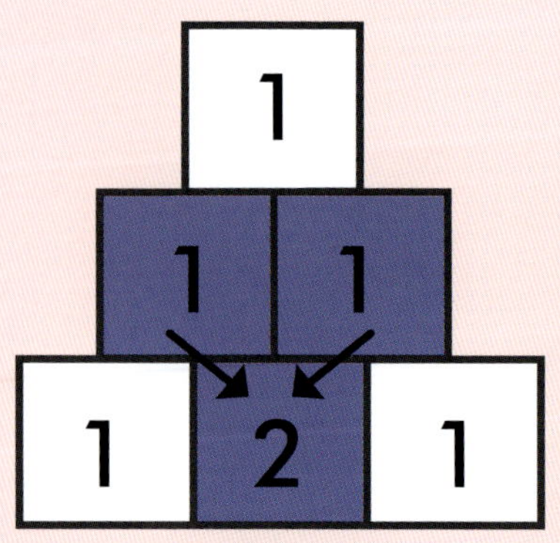

Big-brained Blaise made popular a number pattern known as **PASCAL'S TRIANGLE**. It's built from 1s on the ends of each row but with each number inside created by adding the two numbers directly above it.

It may not look much, but this triangle's a **TREASURE TROVE** of number patterns...

The numbers in the second diagonal column in from each edge are the "natural" or counting numbers.

And that's just the start. Contained within the triangle are neat solutions to some problems in algebra and **PROBABILITY**—an area of math we're going to look at next—what were the chances of that?

WHAT ARE THE CHANCES?

Pascal and others in the 17th and 18th Centuries studied **PROBABILITY**. This is the likelihood of something (called an event) happening—from it raining tomorrow to whether the whole school will go **WILD** for your rendition of Taylor Swift on the recorder during assembly.

Probability can be shown as a number ranging from 1 (will **ABSOLUTELY, DEFINITELY HAPPEN**) to 0 (no chance—as in no chance your recorder performance will impress anyone). This number can also be shown as a **PERCENTAGE**, **FRACTION**, or **ONE IN X** chance.

$$\text{Probability} = \frac{\text{number of ways the event can happen}}{\text{total number of possible outcomes}}$$

Some events can happen in more than one way (for example, you can get 9 with two dice by rolling a 5 and a 4 OR a 6 and a 3).

To work out probability, you ideally need to know all the outcomes. With one die, this is easy. There are six outcomes equally likely and each dice roll is **INDEPENDENT**. So, the probability of rolling a particular number will always be 1 in 6.

Other events are **DEPENDENT**, like picking out a number of cards in a row from a deck. After each card is removed, the probability changes. For example, the probability of picking a diamond card from a full deck is $\frac{13}{52}$ = 0.25 or 1 in 4.

But with that card removed, the chances of picking a diamond next time round is $\frac{12}{51}$

To get the probability of the first three cards picked all being diamonds, you multiply the probability of each card pick together.

$$\frac{13}{52} \times \frac{12}{51} \times \frac{11}{50} = 0.01294 \text{ or } 1.294\%$$

Probability is used to make millions of **PREDICTIONS** each day, such as weather forecasts and trades on stock markets. These predictions are often also made using another branch of mathematics—**STATISTICS**.

STAT ATTACK!

Statistics is all about gathering **INFORMATION** and working out what it tells you. Today, we're bombarded and surrounded by stats for sports, business, health, and the environment...

A few centuries ago, though, there were next-to-no statistics. The only data usually collected back then was gathered by a **CENSUS**. This counted a **COUNTRY'S PEOPLE** and sometimes other assets such as crops or buildings.

One of the first uses of stats was pretty *grim*. A 17th-century London shopkeeper called John Graunt analyzed **BIRTHS** and **DEATHS**. He used the statistics to **PREDICT** how long people would live. His results weren't cool for kids—he estimated that 36 out of 100 children born at the time wouldn't make it to their **SEVENTH BIRTHDAY**.

As the numbers of people on the planet boomed in the 18th and 19th Centuries, businesses, scientists, and governments started collecting more **DATA**. This was so that they could use statistics to make **SUMMARIES**, **ESTIMATES**, and **PREDICTIONS**.

Once collected, data is looked at and analyzed to find **PATTERNS** and other useful information. Often, averages are calculated to give a summary of a set of data. Arithmetical **MEAN** is one type of average. You get it by **ADDING** all the different numbers together and **DIVIDING** the total by the number of numbers.

THE AVERAGE PERSON FARTS 5 TO 10 TIMES PER DAY.

Another type of average is **MODE**. This is the most **COMMONLY OCCURRING** value in a set of data, such as 10 people in a population of 15 all being 1.65m in height.

STATISTICS can be displayed in many ways, from humble facts and figures to pie charts, graphs, bar charts, pictograms, or histograms. Some mathematicians, such as **CARL GAUSS**, found they could also be analyzed in other ways to reveal more information.

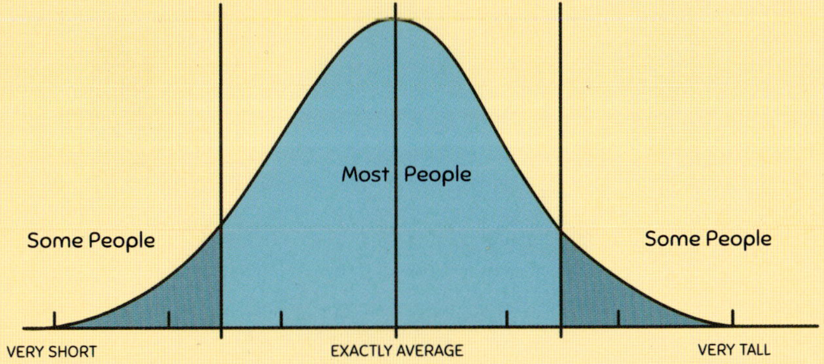

In a normal distribution, most of the values huddle together in the middle part of the graph. The very **CENTER** of the graph is the **ARITHMETIC MEAN**. The further away from the mean, the fewer values you'll find.

Gauss developed the idea about measuring distances from this mean in the middle which he called **MEAN ERROR**. It later became known as **STANDARD DEVIATION**. If your data is normally distributed (so, when plotted on a graph it looks like the bell curve above) then one "standard deviation" contains 68% of all the values in the data set. Two standard deviations include 95% of all the data. If the standard deviation is low, then you know most of the values are close to the mean.

Stats wasn't the only place where clever Carl made his mark. As a teenager, he showed how to create a 17-sided shape called a **HEPTADECAGON**, with all 17 sides the same length. This was a shape thought impossible by math greats such as Euclid and Isaac Newton. Mind you, perhaps Newton was too busy battling another mathematician to investigate fully...

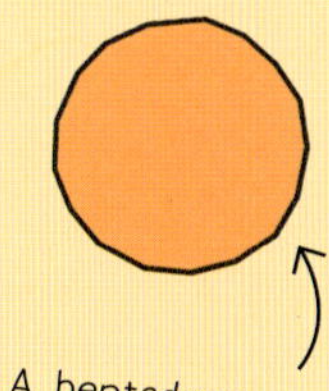
A heptadecagon

THE CALCULUS WARS

Around 320 years ago, a vicious feud broke out between two math legends, over who invented a branch of math called **CALCULUS**.

Sir Isaac 'Gravity Man' Newton

In one corner stood Mr. Gravity himself, British scientist **SIR ISAAC NEWTON**, who had also invented reflecting telescopes and explained the science and math of how objects move. In the other corner, **GOTTFRIED LEIBNIZ**, a brilliant German logician, philosopher, and mathematician. He invented an early calculator machine and pioneered the use of **BINARY NUMBERS** (see pp98–99).

Gottfried 'Lethal Logician' Leibniz

Newton developed his **CALCULUS** system in the 1660s, Leibniz a few years later, but published his system first. Newton claimed Leibniz stole his ideas. Leibniz sniped back, explaining how his calculus was far **SUPERIOR** to Newton's. Other scientists took sides and goaded the two bickering big-brains on, just like a fight in a playground. Oh, grow up!

The feud continued for years, and ended with Leibniz out of favor and Newton getting the credit during his lifetime. Today, **BOTH** are bigged-up as **CO-INVENTORS**. And credit is also now given to earlier math masters, such as **Archimedes** and **Bhāskara II** in India, who also thought up similar ideas.

Why the big fuss?

Well, calculus deals with how equations, quantities, and things **CHANGE** over time or across space. It allows people to **COMPARE** changing amounts, study acceleration (how things ***speed up*** or slow down), calculate changes in prices or costs, and measure how sound and light move in waves.

Calculus would quickly turn out to be a very useful tool in science, engineering, and business, particularly once other mathematicians, like the Swiss whizz, **LEONHARD EULER**, had smoothed out a few wrinkles.

OI OI, EULER!

LEONHARD EULER (pronounced "Oiler") was a math giant and a busy, busy, busy one. This Swiss whizz wrote over **860 BOOKS** and **SCIENTIFIC PAPERS**—an average of 15 per year as an adult—throughout his lifetime (1707–1783).

Euler found ways of combining the best elements of both Leibniz and Newton's versions of **CALCULUS**, making it useful to solve **REAL-WORLD** problems in science and engineering.

But it wasn't just calculus; no area of math seemed safe from his gaze. Euler had a crack at pretty much EVERYTHING.

He popularized using the symbol π for Pi, and the use of x, y, and z as unknown amounts in algebra. He also used the Greek letter, sigma, shown as $\sum$, to describe the sum of a series of numbers.

Legendary Leo developed **GRAPH THEORY** (see page 101) and created important equations about elasticity (how s t r e t c h y something is). These equations were later used by engineers to help build the Eiffel Tower. **C'EST MAGNIFIQUE!**

Do you remember **PLATONIC SOLIDS?** They were back on p28. Well, Euler ALSO discovered a simple rule about them: their number of faces plus their corners and minus their number of edges always equaled two.

Oh, and if that wasn't enough, he not only has an **IRRATIONAL NUMBER** called e or Euler's number, named after him, he did sterling work on **IMAGINARY NUMBERS**.

JUST MY IMAGINATION

By the 16th and 17th Centuries, mathematicians were knee-deep in tricky **FORMULAE** and **EQUATIONS**. Sometimes, they got stuck, such as when facing an equation like $\mathbf{x^2 = -1}$

You see, you cannot square a **REAL NUMBER** (multiply it by itself) and get a negative answer like –1.

An Italian, Rafael Bombelli, decided to put x = √–1 (the square root of –1) as the answer to the above equation. Some fellow mathematicians weren't that impressed! Frenchman René Descartes labeled √–1 unkindly as an "**IMAGINARY NUMBER**." The name stuck and it's now shortened to i.

Multiples of i can be used. For example, 2i is the square root of –4 and 3i the square root of –9.

WHAT'S THE POINT?

Well, some important equations require a cheeky $\sqrt{-1}$ or some other square root of a **MINUS NUMBER** to make them work. Such equations are used to measure the flow of **ELECTRICITY** and in math models of how air flows over an aircraft's wings. Important stuff.

Now, did you have an imaginary friend when you were younger? If you still have one, don't be embarrassed. Mine's called Wilfred and he often hangs around to compliment me… well, someone has to.

COMPLEX NUMBERS are basically a real number with an imaginary friend attached, such as 11 – 4i or 6 + 0.7i. I know, bamboozling, isn't it?

Don't worry if you're confused. All you need to know is that complex numbers are used lots in **PHYSICS** and **ENGINEERING**. They were developed by some mighty mathematicians including legendary Leonhard Euler who also created **EULER DIAGRAMS**—an early way of showing what we now call "sets."

GET SET, GO!

SETS are basically collections of things—numbers or objects—with shared properties. They allow comparisons between different information to be made and are used in statistics and probability. German mathematician, **GEORG CANTOR** was a pioneer, writing about set theory in 1874.

Contained within curly brackets are the different elements of a set, each separated by a comma. So, a set containing things I ate today could be

A = {eggs, banana, apple, toast, pasta, orange, fingernails, ice cream}

Urgh, I know - a terrible habit

Set B contains fruit I ate today, B = (banana, apple, orange). It forms a set within a set, called a subset, and is written as B ⊂ A.

Things I ate today:

A union (written as $A \cup B$) is all things in two or more sets.

If two sets share some but not all elements they're said to **INTERSECT**. So, if set A contained all whole numbers between 1 and 10 and set B contained all the numbers you can divide by 3, then the two sets intersect and $A \cap B = \{3, 6, 9\}$.

VENN DIAGRAMS are visual ways of showing sets, making it easier to see intersections and other comparisons. They were in-Venn-ted (sorry) by British mathematician John Venn in 1880.

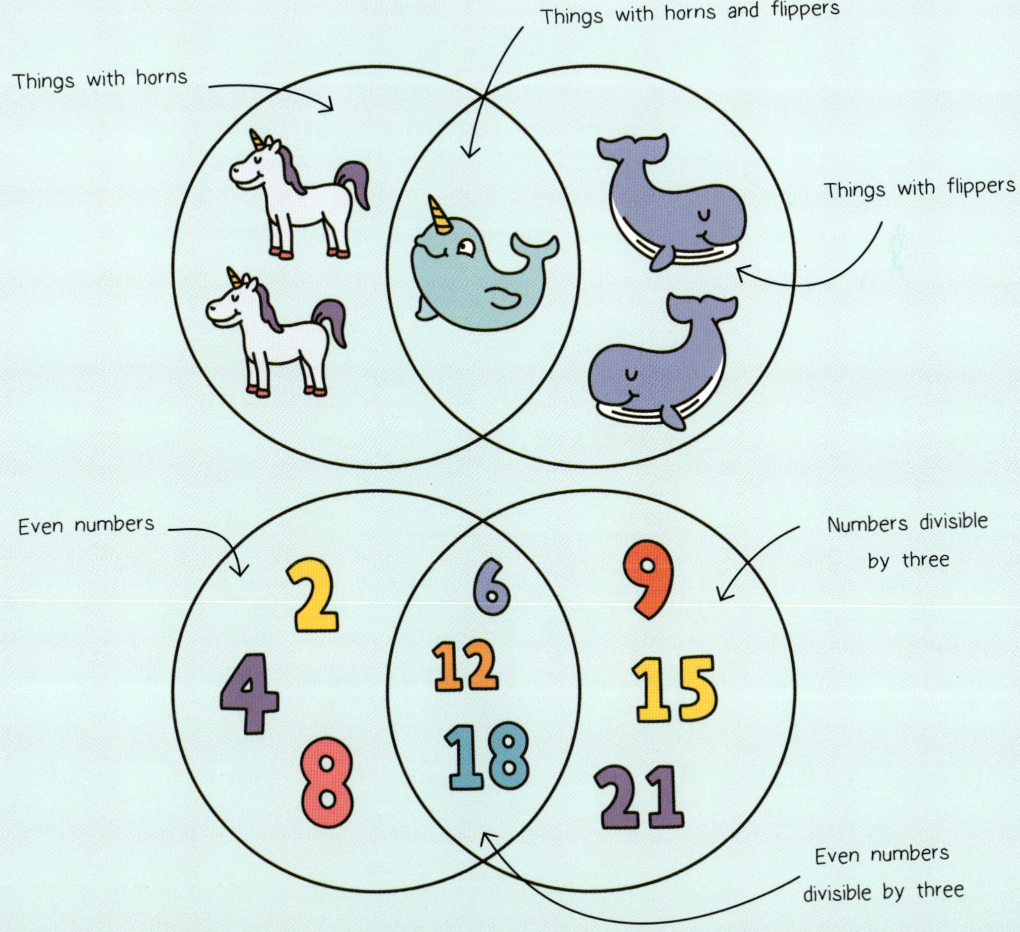

COMPUTERS IN SKIRTS

Mathematical tables for science, transport, and engineering were all the rage in the 18th and 19th Centuries. These were produced by teams of human math nuts known as **COMPUTERS**! Many were women who slaved away for hours...

and hours...

and... you get the point.

Some, like **MARY EDWARDS** and her daughter **ELIZA** in England, calculated tables of data to help ships navigate. Others produced statistics or—like the team of all-female computers who worked at Harvard Observatory in the USA—performed math for **ASTRONOMERS**.

Human errors crept into some tables, which annoyed those who used them. One, British engineer **CHARLES BABBAGE**, decided to do something about it.

He tried to build mechanical computers out of thousands and thousands of gears and other parts made of brass and iron. His most ambitious machine —the **ANALYTICAL ENGINE**—was to be powered by a steam engine.

Babbage's pal, **ADA LOVELACE**, was a countess who counted. A budding mathematician, she wrote a series of instructions for the Analytical Engine to produce number sequences and solve math problems, making her the world's first **COMPUTER PROGRAMMER**.

The **ANALYTICAL ENGINE** was never completed, but 90 years later, the first working computers were built. And guess what.

What?

They also used female human computers to function, but instead of gears, these machines relied on **ELECTRICITY**, **LOGIC GATES**, and **BINARY NUMBERS**.

BRILLIANT BINARY

Babbage's mechanical computers were designed to use **BASE 10** numbers, the kind we count with, but when electronic computers finally arrived, they used **BASE 2** (also known as **BINARY NUMBERS**) instead.

The binary number system, remember, was explained by that German genius **GOTTFRIED LEIBNIZ** back in the 17th Century. He in turn had been inspired by a 3,000-year-old Chinese text, the I Ching. The I Ching was used to tell the future: readers would randomly generate patterns made up of **YIN** (broken lines) or **YANG** (unbroken lines), and the patterns created corresponded to various meanings described in the I Ching.

Leibniz saw that even the most complicated meanings could be simplified right down to patterns of just yin and yang. Likewise, the binary number system only contains two different values: **ONE** and **ZERO**.

In the binary system, the place values **DOUBLE** each time, like this:

64	32	16	8	4	2	1

So, in order to write the number 9 for example you'd put a 1 in the 8s column, 0s in the 4 and 2 columns, and a 1 in the 1s column, like this, 1001:

64	32	16	8	4	2	1
			1	0	0	1

Or, to write 43, you'd put 1 in the 32s, 0 in the 16s, 1 in the 8s, 0 in the 4s, and 1 in both the 2s and the 1s, like this: 101011

Why is this useful for **COMPUTERS?** Well, engineers found that binary numbers could be represented by electricity flowing around electrical circuits. An "**ON**" signal equaled 1 and no signal (electricity **OFF**) equaled 0.

THROUGH THE LOGIC GATE

In the 1850s, there was an English know-it-all called **GEORGE BOOLE**. He *loved* school so much, he opened his own in Lincoln, England, at the age of 19. He also taught himself Greek, French, German, and Italian, and developed his own system of simple algebra—called "**BOOLEAN LOGIC**"—which worked perfectly with **BINARY**. The answers in Boolean logic are always 1 or 0.

Boolean logic was used in the 1920s and '30s to make types of electrical switch called a **LOGIC GATE**. Each gate received a signal (called the **INPUT**) and made a simple on or off decision (called the **OUTPUT**).

These switches, or gates, have names such as **NOT** gates, **AND** gates, and **OR** gates.

With a **NOT GATE**, there is one input, and the output is the **OPPOSITE** of the input. So, for example, if an "on" signal (in binary, a 1) reaches a NOT gate, the gate's output will be the opposite, an "off" or 0 signal.

With an **AND GATE**, there are two inputs, and only one output. **BOTH** inputs have to be the same in order to turn the output signal on.

With an **OR GATE**, there are also two inputs. At least one of them has to be an "on" signal or a 1, in order for the output to be on.

By itself, a single logic gate isn't much to write home about, but when many were linked together in **ELECTRIC CIRCUITS**, they could perform math at sparkling ***speed***. Suddenly, truly awesome and useful computers were just around the corner...

MACHINE MATH

In 1938, **KONRAD ZUSE** completed the world's first working computer, the Z1, in his parents' apartment in Berlin. It contained **30,000 PARTS** and used binary numbers to make its calculations.

When World War II began the following year, the demand grew for lots of deadly math for new weapon designs and to help plot the paths of artillery shells so they landed on target. In the USA and Europe, BIG computers like **ENIAC** and **COLOSSUS** were built to perform this sort of math.

ENIAC weighed nearly 30 tons—five elephants' worth—and was the size of a basketball court. It could take days to rewire the machine each time it needed to run a new program… but when it ran, it was ***lightning fast***. Whoosh!

It took a human computer **15–20 HOURS** to calculate the path of a single artillery shell. ENIAC completed the task in just **30 SECONDS**.

In the 1950s and 1960s, computers started shrinking fast. All their electric circuits and logic gates were shrunk onto tiny wafers known as **SILICON CHIPS**. In 1995, all of ENIAC's computing power and abilities were fitted onto a single chip smaller than your fingernail.

Computers not only got smaller, they also became far cheaper, faster, and MUCH more **POWERFUL**.

Modern computers can perform **MILLIONS** of calculations in less than a blink of an eye. They've helped free up mathematicians from heavy number-crunching so they can think creatively about brand new **THEORIES**.

FUNKY THEORIES

As math has advanced, spurred on at times by computers, it's sprouted more new ideas and theories, some of which are pretty **FAR OUT**. Here are three of the **FUNKIEST**.

GAME THEORY

How people make **DECISIONS** in a situation can be studied using math according to this theory. The "game" people play in **GAME THEORY** can actually be a strategy game like chess or something deadly serious like a business negotiation or a war. Game theory builds mathematical models to work out whether people should **COMPETE** against one another or **WORK TOGETHER**.

CHAOS THEORY

In 1961, a computer simulation of the weather produced different outcomes each time it ran. It led a puzzled US math man, **EDWARD LORENZ**, to develop chaos theory.

This shows how the behavior of really **COMPLICATED** systems like the weather or population growth cannot be measured and predicted perfectly by math. Why? Because we cannot know every single thing that is happening. Even the tiniest variation in one small part can cause **BIG** changes elsewhere.

GRAPH THEORY

While trying to find a route that crossed seven bridges in a Russian city, legendary Leo (Leonhard Euler) kicked off **GRAPH THEORY**. Confusingly, this isn't about graphs such as bar charts that show statistics. Instead, these graphs are more like **MAPS**, being collections of lines and points (called **NODES**) to map out **RELATIONSHIPS** between things such as distances between points, or who knows whom in a group of people.

Coders sometimes use graph theory when designing algorithms for computer programs or mapping out the different parts of a **COMPUTER NETWORK**.

BIG DATA

Computers are now found everywhere and I do mean **EVERYWHERE**. Your home can contain dozens, many hidden inside smart appliances, tablets, and smartphones. What's more, lots of these gadgets can **SHARE INFORMATION** with each other.

That's just the start.

Perhaps without realizing it, you and all the other billions of computer users around the globe, create **HUGE** amounts of data when liking, swiping, or posting on social media, using the Internet, buying online, or uploading pics and vids.

In any two days in 2018, people created as much data as the entire human population produced from the beginning of time until the year 2000. **WOWZERS!**

Much of this **DATA** is collected and kept at places called server farms. They contain thousands of data storage computers. **BIG DATA** is all about analyzing the information they contain, using math, to find useful information such as **PATTERNS** and **TRENDS**.

Who uses **BIG DATA**?

Good question, and one with lots of answers:

- governments to learn more about their country's people and their needs
- doctors to try to spot health problems early
- businesses to identify what their customers will buy

Data is even being used by law enforcement agencies to predict and prevent **CRIME**. Trends in where crimes are committed, and by who, are analyzed by data programs, and extra police are sent out to monitor those areas. However, using data in this way is controversial, because errors in the analysis can lead to people and places being unfairly or wrongly targeted.

Big Data is only going to get **BIGGER**. In the future, more and more info about you and the world will be analyzed in increasingly clever ways and may yield amazing new discoveries.

FUTURE MATH

Even with all the work being done with Big Data and predictions, no one truly knows what will happen to math in the **FUTURE**, and anyone who says they do know is lying!

What we can do is make some educated **GUESSES**. So, here are three.

Future computers may be able to truly **UNDERSTAND** mathematical knowledge and theorems and play around with them to come up with **NEW IDEAS**. This could mean that the next big breakthrough in math is made by a machine, not a human being.

As Big Data gets **BIGGER**, the future may see math accurately predict **RISKS** and warn of dangers and disasters well in advance. With so much information to process, we may become more and more reliant on machines to do the learning and analysis for us.

There'll still be room for top human mathematicians to dazzle us all with new theories, though... perhaps by **YOU**!

Whole new **THEOREMS** and areas of math may be discovered in this century or the next that change everything! Future math, for example, may explain more about how the Universe works, and may lead us to travel farther into **SPACE**.

What is **CERTAIN** (a 1 in 1 chance) is that math will continue to play a **VITAL** part in people's lives.

Timeline Of Math Discoveries

Human beings have learned a lot about math since we first started counting on **FINGERS** and **BABOONS** all those thousands of years ago. Here's a quick recap of math over the ages.

43,000 BCE

The Lebombo bone is the first confirmed example of numbers being recorded as notches on a bone, a device known as a tally stick.

3,100 BCE

A fully developed number system is used by this time by the Sumerians in Mesopotamia. Within a few Centuries, scholars were copying out times tables onto clay tablets.

212 BCE

Great Greek mathematician and inventor, Archimedes dies after a lifetime of discovery, including working out formulae for the areas of various shapes.

C.200 BCE

Written on bamboo strips, The Writings on Reckonings summarizes lots of ancient Chinese math breakthroughs including working with fractions.

C.100 CE

The ancient Chinese learn how to make paper, allowing math theorems and working out to be easily written down and passed on to others.

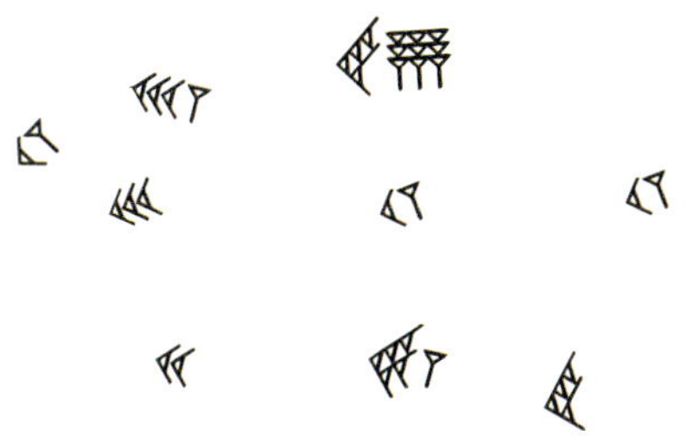

1,830 BCE

The Babylonian civilization uses a number system based on 60s.

2,700 BCE

The ancient Egyptians use math in the construction of their mighty pyramids.

300 BCE

Euclid summarizes all the known math of shapes and angles, known as geometry, in writings that would influence other math men and women for centuries.

530 BCE

Pythagoras opens a school where mathematicians and others flock to learn and discuss matters. The Pythagoreans develop many math theorems.

400 CE

Roman mathematician Hypatia becomes the first known female head of a school of math and philosophy, based in Alexandria.

628 CE

Indian thinker Brahmagupta defines zero as a number itself rather than just being a gap or hole in a larger number.

762 CE

The city of Baghdad is founded and becomes home to a great library and learning center for math and other subjects, known as the House of Wisdom. Great advances in algebra, geometry, and other math occurs there.

1299

The rulers of the Italian city-state of Florence are so terrified of the new number, zero, they ban it!

1557

Welshman Robert Recorde introduces the equal sign (=), which becomes popular in arithmetic and equations.

1618

Eccentric Scotsman John Napier introduces his system of logarithms to speed up calculating big numbers. Tables of logarithms become used by sailors, engineers, scientists, and businesspeople.

820 CE

House of Wisdom director, al-Khwarizmi, writes the Al-jabr, explaining ways to use algebra more effectively and practically. This branch of mathematics is named in his honor.

1202

Italian merchant and math man Fibonacci writes his book promoting the use of Hindu-Arabic numbers instead of Roman numerals and introduces the Fibonacci sequence of numbers to the world.

1654

Twelve years after building an early mechanical calculator, Frenchman Blaise Pascal, along with Pierre de Fermat, develops the theory of probability.

1720
Leonhard Euler enrolls at Basel University. He's only 13 at the time! In the decades that follow, Euler will develop graph theory, improve calculus and mathematical analysis, and write hundreds of papers and books.

1841
Ada, Countess of Lovelace, writes instructions for Charles Babbage's Analytical Engine, considered to be the world's first computer program.

1945
The giant computer ENIAC begins running in the USA. It is capable of performing in seconds math that had previously taken people many hours to figure out.

1970
The first electronic pocket calculators appear, designed and built by Japanese companies including Sharp, Canon, and Sanyo.

1991
The first websites on the World Wide Web are made available to the public. Now, people can share their knowledge and interests, including math, with the whole world.

1854

George Boole introduces his system of logic, which works with binary numbers. Boolean logic will become an important part of computing in the 20th Century.

1928

John von Neumann wrote a paper that would form an important part of Game Theory.

1938

Young German engineer Konrad Zuse builds the Z1—the first working computer using binary numbers. Five years later, it is destroyed during an air raid.

2011

Twenty years on from the World Wide Web's birth, there are over 345 million websites.

2019

Using a powerful computer program, Japanese math expert Emma Haruka Iwao produces the most accurate value of Pi so far. The number is 31.4 trillion digits long!

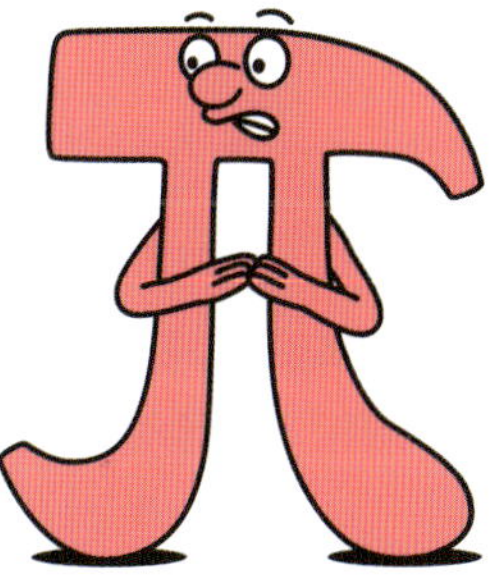

WHEN MATH GOES WRONG...

This book is packed with great examples of **BRILLIANT** mathematicians performing amazingly accurate math, but what happens when ~~misshtakkes~~, sorry, mistakes are made?

Much of the time, bad math is checked, spotted, and corrected, but sometimes it gets released into the wild... with potentially **DEVASTATING** results.

If your mental arithmetic isn't that good, you might find yourself buying one of these **UNFORTUNATE OFFERS** or short-changed at a store or market. You may not realize that you have been **OVERCHARGED** for your purchases before it's too late. Most likely, you've lost pennies, but some mistakes cost much, much MORE.

In 2003, a trader at a Japanese finance firm called Mizuho Securities got his numbers in a muddle. Instead of selling one share for 610,000 yen (about $5,500), he sold 610,000 shares at a price of one yen each. This blunder cost the company a cool **$240 MILLION**!

Across the **PACIFIC OCEAN**, there were red faces in Canada in 2018 when one political party's budget math made a mistake by adding, not taking away, a big figure. The mistake totaled $1.4 billion!

When Spain was designing its new S80 **SUBMARINES**, someone put a decimal point in the wrong place. As a result, the sub would dive, but was too **heavy** to rise to the surface. Whoops.

The sub had to be lengthened by 30 feet, costing millions and millions, but then it wouldn't fit into its dock—**DOUBLE TROUBLE**! It cost another $26 million just to increase the size of the dock. Mind you, this wasn't as bad as what happened to the most powerful warship in the world all the way back in 1628...

MORE MATH MISTAKES

In 1628, the pride of Sweden's navy, the **VASA**, was launched, sailed just 1,400 yards, toppled over, and sank!

The ship was poorly designed, too top-heavy, and built with workers using **DIFFERENT MEASUREMENTS**. Some worked in 11 in. long units, others in 12 in., so the rulers used to measure parts of the ships were all different lengths. Oh dear.

Other **MEASURING MIX-UPS** have also caused problems, including an airliner running out of fuel 40,000 ft above ground. The Air Canada Boeing 767 was refueled in **POUNDS** but had been checked before take-off, assuming the fuel was in **KILOGRAMS**. As there are 2.2 pounds to a kilo, it meant that the plane had less than **HALF** the fuel it needed.

Luckily, the pilot managed to glide the plane down safely, but another metric mix-up saw the loss of an entire sparkling new spacecraft.

The **MARS CLIMATE ORBITER** was a $130 million NASA project that whizzed through space for ten months in 1999, got ever so close to Mars, and then broke up before it could do any exploring.

Space investigators found that some of the computer code controlling the craft was written using **METRIC** units, while other programs were in **IMPERIAL** (pounds, feet, and inches). No one had thought to check or convert between the two. **D'OH!**

Another computer math error saw the US Navy's brand new Smart Ship, **USS YORKTOWN** unable to move for a few hours in 1997. Someone had entered a zero by mistake and when the computer tried to divide by zero, it caused an embarrassing shutdown.

MENTAL MATH

Maths puzzles and riddles can not only teach you something, they can also be lots of fun. Why not try out these puzzlers (without looking at the answers on pp122–123)?

PLUS SIGN

Can you arrange these shapes to form a plus sign?

SHAPING UP

Which number is the highest—the number of sides of an octagon or the number of diagonals in a hexagon?

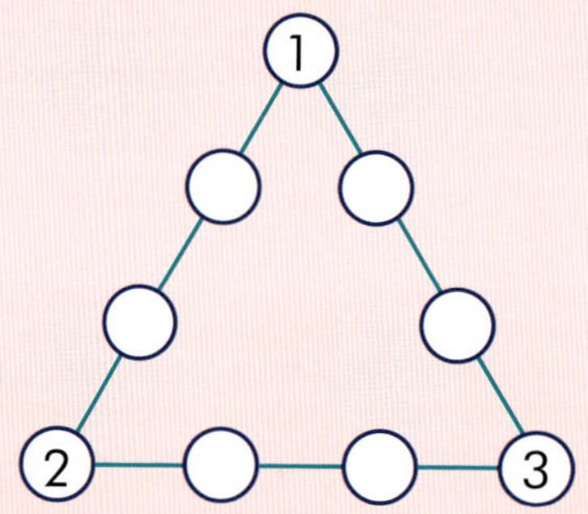

TRIANGULAR TEASER

Add the numbers 4–9 into the circles so that each side of the triangle adds up to the same number. Can you work out what that number will be?

SUPER SHORT RIDDLE

A half is a sixth of it. What is it?

UP 'N' DOWN

Make a triangle of coins like here. Now, only moving three coins, can you change the direction the triangle points in from up to down?

PLUS AND MINUS

Add plus and minus signs between the following numbers to complete the sum.

14   11   5   3   9 = 26

WINNING TICKET

A raffle has 20 prizes and 80 customers who each buy two tickets. What is the probability of a particular ticket winning a prize?

MAKING THE MOST

You are really hungry and love cakes. Which offer gives you the most sweet treats?

$8\frac{1}{3}$ cakes   8.35 cakes $\frac{68}{8}$ cakes

KAPREKAR'S CONSTANT

Crazy name, crazy puzzle. Get a friend to choose a four-digit number. This number must have at least two different digits, so 9,999 is out, but numbers like 1,337 or 2,488 are fine.

1. Arrange the four digits in descending order with the biggest digit first.
2. Then arrange the four digits again in ascending order with the smallest digit first.
3. Take away the smaller number from the biggest number.
4. Repeat the first three steps until you keep on getting the same number. What is it?

ANSWERS

Here are the answers to the puzzles on the previous page.
If you haven't tried them yet—no peeking!

PLUS SIGN

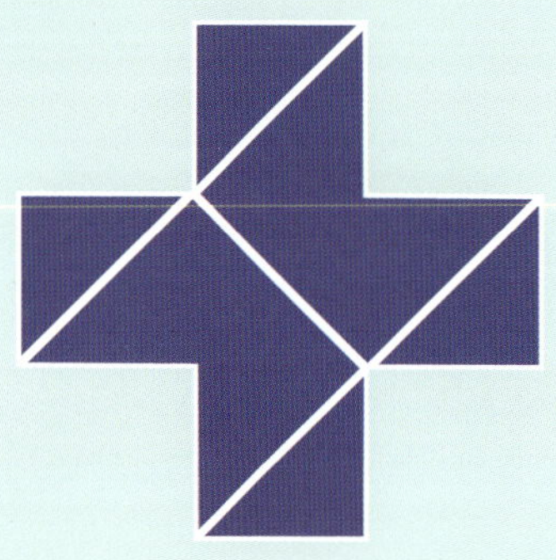

SHAPING UP

Hexagon has more diagonals (nine) than an octagon has sides (eight)

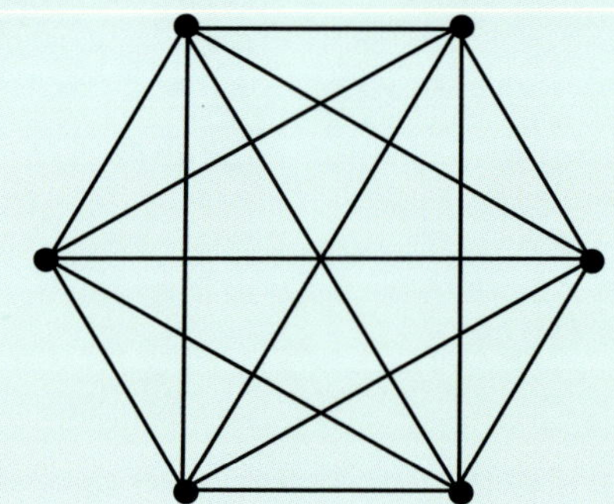

TRIANGULAR TEASER

The answer is 17.

SUPER SHORT RIDDLE

3 $(6 \times \frac{1}{2} = 3)$

UP 'N' DOWN

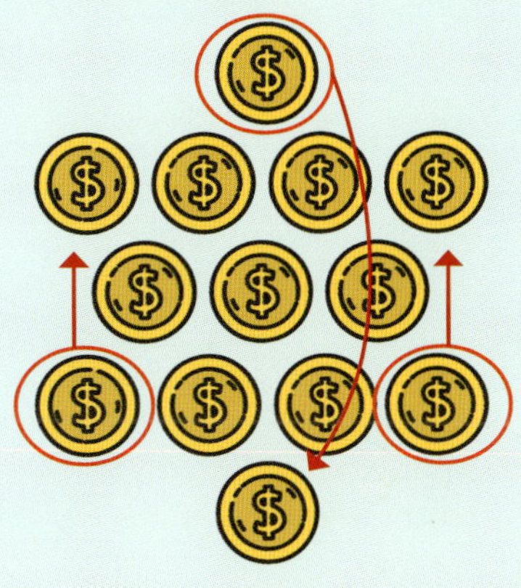

PLUS AND MINUS

14 + 11 - 5 – 3 + 9 = 26

WINNING TICKET

A 1 in 8 chance (160 tickets divided by 20 prizes).

MAKING THE MOST

$\frac{68}{8}$ cakes which equals 8.5 cakes

KAPREKAR'S CONSTANT

6174

Whatever number chosen at the start, once you get to 6,174 you're stuck in a loop with 7,641 – 1,467 = 6,174. This number is known as Kaprekar's Constant after the Indian mathematician, D. R. Kaprekar.

GLOSSARY

ALGEBRA A branch of math that uses letters and symbols to represent numbers. It is used to find unknown values and to create math models of real-world situations.

BINARY The base 2 number system with numbers made up of 1 or 0.

CIRCUMFERENCE The measurement all the way around the outside edge of a circle.

DENOMINATOR The bottom part of a fraction.

DIAMETER The distance across a circle, which passes through the center.

DISTRIBUTION Often used in statistics to describe how data is shared or spread out.

EQUATION Two expressions that have the same value, separated by an equal (=) sign such as $4x = 12$ or $2x + 8 = 4y$.

FORMULA A group of mathematical symbols and numbers that show how to work something out.

GEOMETRY A branch of math that deals with shapes, objects, lines, points and angles.

HINDU-ARABIC NUMBER SYSTEM The name given to the numbers we use today, made up of the different numerals 0–9.

HYPOTENUSE The longest side of a right-angled triangle.

INFINITY A number that doesn't end, so cannot be measured precisely.

MEAN A type of average found by adding up a list of numbers and dividing by how many numbers are in the list.

NEGATIVE NUMBER A number less than zero.

PERCENTAGE A number or ratio shown as a fraction of 100. So, 8 percent (or 8 %) is the same as writing $\frac{8}{100}$.

PLACE VALUE The value of each digit of a number. So, when you write 72, the place value of the 7 means 70.

POLYGON A two-dimensional (2D) shape made from straight lines, such as a triangle, square, or pentagon.

PRIME NUMBER A number greater than one that cannot be divided evenly by any number other than itself or one.

PROBABILITY The likelihood of something happening.

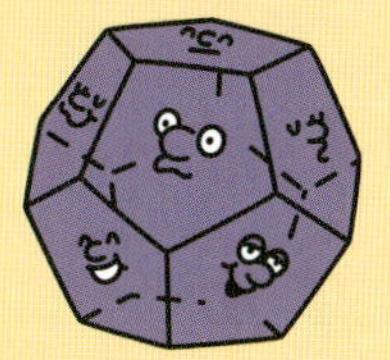

RADIUS The distance from the center of a circle to its circumference.

SEQUENCE A list of numbers that follows a pattern.

SQUARE A square of a number is that number multiplied by itself. So two squared equals four.

SQUARE ROOT The square root of a number is a value that, when it's multiplied by itself, equals the original number. So, the square root of nine is three (3 x 3 = 9).

SYMMETRICAL An object or some other thing which is exactly the same on both sides.

VOLUME The amount an object can hold. For example, a bathtub may have a volume of 35 gallons of water or a box may contain a space measured at 1.5 cubed feet.

INDEX

First published in 2020 by Wide Eyed Editions, an imprint of The Quarto Group.
100 Cummings Center, Suite 265D, Beverly, MA 01915, USA.
T +1 978-282-9590 **www.QuartoKnows.com**

A CIP record for this book is available from the Library of Congress.
ISBN 978-0-7112-4903-5
eISBN 978-0-7112-6335-2
The illustrations were created artwork created with digital media
Set in Futura

Published by Georgia Amson-Bradshaw
Designed by Myrto Dimitrakoulia
Edited by Georgia Amson-Bradshaw
Production by Dawn Cameron

Manufactured in Guangdong, China TT012021

1 3 5 7 9 8 6 4 2

CLEVER CARL AND THE SPREAD OF STATS

Carl Gauss was so good at math that he was correcting his father's accounts before he was **FIVE YEARS OLD**. Say whaaaaat?!

Gauss was fascinated by the **DISTRIBUTION** of data. This is all about how the different values in a statistical sample, such as all the heights of kids in a class, are spread out.

He found that many sets of data are **NORMALLY DISTRIBUTED**. This meant that if all the values were plotted on a graph, they form a symmetrical shape called a **GAUSSIAN CURVE**. It's also known as a **BELL CURVE** because the graph may look like a bit like a church bell.